The Bible and Sexuality

A Course Reader

Karen R. Keen

Contemplatio Publishing
Durham, North Carolina 27717
contemplatiopublishing.com

ISBN 978-1-7348326-1-7

For my students.
Your questions inspire me.

Contents

Preface

What did you learn about sex and the Christian life while growing up in church or as an adult? Was your experience similar to mine? One memory that stands out is a high school youth group discussion on sex. It was a Wednesday night and the pastor put lyrics of popular radio songs on the overhead projector to counsel us about problematic music. He discussed the lyrics of "Pour Some Sugar on Me" by Def Leppard, explaining its inappropriate innuendos and why we should be careful about what we listen to. My parents echoed this concern, particularly when it came to Madonna.

They were right, of course, no fifteen-year-old needs to be exposed to graphic depictions of sex. But their concerns did little to address the questions my friends and I had about that forbidden fruit. We knew we weren't supposed to have sex before marriage or engage with lewd media. But curiosity and youthful desire had us talking among ourselves about the meaning of sex and the best way to navigate life as sexual beings.

Since my formative years in the 1980s and 90s, the conversation on sexuality has only amplified. Churches are still trying to discern how to best guide parishioners toward a Christ-centered sexual ethic. Not only are ministry leaders addressing non-marital sex, but also grappling with broader pressing questions. What did the biblical authors think about sexuality and why? What is the meaning of marriage? Are the prohibitions against same-sex relations in Scripture applicable today? Is it possible for people to live in life-long celibacy? Is polyamory acceptable, given that polygamy is sanctioned by God in the Old Testament? What does healthy dating look like?

In response to the need for meaningful Christian contemplation on the topic of sex, I created The Bible and Sexuality class, for which this present volume was designed. The course covers sexual ethics broadly, with emphasis on the question of same-sex relationships. A distinctive of the class is teaching students to craft an overarching ethical framework, as well as discern their method of biblical interpretation. Participants from a variety of theological viewpoints have attended, including pastors and ministry leaders discerning church policy and pastoral care.

The Bible and Sexuality: A Course Reader is an anthology of essays, some of them initially published on my blogs and updated for the present volume. It includes two primary sections. The first addresses descriptive ethics. That is, the biblical authors' moral reasoning in their time and place. Essays cover the biblical authors' views on sexual morality, verses on same-sex relations, and principles for biblical interpretation. The second section addresses normative sexual ethics, focusing on how we apply Scripture to our lives today.

As a course reader, the book is designed to supplement a teacher's lectures and my first book, *Scripture, Ethics, and the Possibility of Same-Sex Relationships* (a required text for the class). However, the essays are also useful as stand-alone texts for anyone curious to explore what it means to have a Christian sexual ethic.

May God's wisdom and grace guide you in all things.

Karen R. Keen, Th.M.
The Redwood Center for Spiritual Care and Education

Part 1: Descriptive Ethics

Understanding the biblical authors' sexual ethics in their socio-historical context.

1

What Does the Bible Say about Sex? A Historical Overview

In antiquity, there was no dating culture like we have in the present-day West, and the parameters for sexual activity were different for men than women.[1] As with the rest of the ancient Near East and Greco-Roman world, women's sexuality was reserved for marriage.[2] In contrast to women, a conservative sexual ethic for Jewish men apparently did not develop until around the 3rd century BCE. By the time of Jesus and Paul, both men and women in Jewish communities were expected to reserve sex for marriage. Tracing Jewish

[1] In addition to sources listed in the footnotes, this essay particularly draws from Karen Keen, "Sexuality, Critical Issues," *Lexham Bible Dictionary*, eds. John D. Barry and Lazarus Wentz (Bellingham, WA: Logos Bible Software, 2014); William Loader, *Making Sense of Sex: Attitudes Toward Sexuality in Early Jewish and Christian Literature* (Grand Rapids: Eerdmans, 2013).

[2] Important to keep in mind is that Song of Songs does not depict a cultural practice of dating, even though the figures in the story are not portrayed as married. The ancient world was highly patricentric and girls' sexuality, across cultures, was guarded to ensure legitimate patrimonial lines. It may have been sung or recited for wedding banquets.

sexual ethics within its historical context is important for understanding sexual ethics in the Bible.

In ancient Hebrew culture, men could lawfully have sex with female slaves and concubines even while married (Gen 16:1–4, 6; 30:3–12; 2 Sam 15:16; 1 Chr 3:9; see also Judg 19:1).[3] Prostitution was frowned upon by some biblical authors (e.g. Prov 6:26), but no law banned the practice. If a man had sex with an unbetrothed girl who was not a slave, concubine, or prostitute, he could be required to marry her (otherwise the girl was likely to be unmarriageable). This was true even if he raped her (Deut 22:28–29; see also 2 Sam 13:1–21).

Men could also marry more than one wife. Israelite law regulated the practice, instructing what constituted an acceptable polygynous union (Exod 21:10–11; Deut 21:15–17). While polygyny was probably rare among the average male, a man might take a second wife if his first spouse was ill or infertile. A wealthy man, however, could afford more wives. Sometimes the scarcity of men during periods of war or disaster fostered the practice (Isa 4:1). Polygynous men in the Bible include, among many others, Jacob, Moses, Elkanah, and David. The prophet Nathan says God gave David multiple wives

---

[3] A female slave given to another male slave as a "wife" did not belong to him. She remained the property of the owner; she and the children were not necessarily freed when the male slave obtained freedom (Exod 21:2–6). See discussion in Raymond Westbrook, "*The Female Slave*," in *Gender and Law in the Hebrew Bible and the Ancient Near East*, edited by V. H. Matthews, et al. (New York: T&T Clark, 2004), 235–37. Similarly, Hagar is still considered Sarah's slave even after being given to Abraham to bear children. Thus, Abraham allows Sarah to expel Hagar because Hagar does not have equal status as a true wife. According to Levitical law if a man had sex with a female slave who was promised to another man, he was not punished with death as normally would be required of adultery. Her status as a slave made it a lesser offense (Lev 19:20–22).

as an act of favor and victory over Saul (2 Sam 12:8). His marriage to Abigail, a godly woman, is also a positive portrayal of polygyny (1 Sam 25).

Israelite women married shortly after puberty in their teens. A woman was expected to be a virgin on her wedding day and provide proof of it (Deut 22:13–21). After marriage, she could only have sex with her husband. Adultery was defined differently for women and men. For women, any extramarital sex constituted adultery. For men, adultery meant having sex with a woman betrothed or married to another man. It was not adultery if he had sex with a slave, concubine, prostitute, or second wife, so long as the women did not belong to another man. In the case of adultery, both parties could be put to death (vv. 23–24).

Jewish male sexuality became more restricted by the 3rd century BCE. By this time, the Greeks had introduced monogamous marriage to the ancient world. Ancient Jewish writings from Qumran (Dead Sea Scrolls) argue against polygyny by using the story of Noah and the ark: the animals entered two by two. Other Jewish writings, including Sirach (23:18), Josephus's *Against Apion* (2.201), and Jubilees (25:4–7) all suggest sexual exclusivity for men in a way not found in the Old Testament.

Increasingly, not only were Jewish men expected to have one wife, but also avoid sex with slaves, concubines, and prostitutes. Philo, a Jewish theologian who lived around the time of Jesus and Paul in the 1st century CE, claimed that unlike the other nations, Jewish men did not have sex until marriage (Philo, *On the Life of Joseph* 9 [43]).

Thus, at the time the New Testament was written, Jews expected men and women to reserve all sexual activity for marriage. Paul clearly held this view. He did not see an outlet for sexual release apart from marriage, rejecting sex with prostitutes (1 Cor 6:15–16) and urging marriage for men who were tempted by sexual activity even with the woman to whom they were betrothed (7:36–38; see also 7:2–4; 8–9).

While Jewish sexual ethics gradually became more conservative for men over time, Greco-Roman customs were still similar to ancient Israelite practice. Men could have sex with slaves, concubines, and prostitutes. At the same time, young women's sexuality was closely guarded. Roman law mandated the death penalty for men who propositioned women that were not prostitutes or slaves. Appolladorus (c. 180–120 BCE) cited three categories of women: "courtesan" (high class prostitute) for pleasure, "concubine" for daily care, and "wife" for legitimate offspring (*Against Neaera,* [Demosthenes] 59.122). Respectable Greco-Roman women reserved sex only for their husbands. Failure to do so resulted in second-class status as a prostitute.

In the early church, bringing together Jewish Christians and Gentile Christians was a challenge for a variety of reasons, including different sexual ethics. One can imagine the Gentiles were perceived as a potential bad influence on Jewish Christians. Notably, when Paul writes about sexual immorality, he is often writing to predominantly Greco-Roman congregations. Jewish Christians already had a conservative sexual ethic that reserved sex for marriage. Similarly, respectable Greco-Roman women did not have sex outside of marriage. The primary problem appears to have been Gentile male converts who were accustomed to being able to have non-marital sex.

All the first Christians were Jews and there was some debate about whether or not Gentiles could even become part of the Christian family. The Jerusalem Council around 50 CE (Acts 15) debated Gentile inclusion. But, despite disagreement, all agreed that Gentile converts should abstain from *porneia* (15:20, 29; 21:5). In the 1st century *porneia* referred to sexual immorality in general.[4] But given what we know about context and sexual ethics among Greeks and Romans, the concern was probably directed primarily towards Gentile male converts, as well as concubines or prostitutes. Significantly, men (more than women) are frequently the subject of Paul's directives on sexual conduct. For example, he singles out men's behavior toward their betrothed and conduct with prostitutes (1 Cor 6 and 7).

Notably, the Jerusalem Council was made up of all Jewish Christians of whom Paul was only one. Paul is not the source of the sexual ethics in the New Testament. Rather these ethics were characteristic of Jews in the 1st century. That is probably why Jesus does not speak about *porneia* as much as Paul, and why Jesus tends to focus on *porneia* related to divorce or lust of the eye and condition of the heart. Jews at this time were not engaging in the same sexual practices as the Gentiles and Jesus was ministering primarily to fellow Jews. In contrast, Paul was reaching out to Gentiles.

While Gentiles did not have to submit to circumcision and other aspects of Torah, they were expected to convert to Jewish sexual ethics. The earliest writing of the New Testament is 1 Thessalonians, penned by Paul shortly after the Jerusalem Council decision (and about 20 years after Jesus's death). This letter states, "For this is the will of God, your sanctification: that you abstain from *porneia,* that each one of you know how to control your own body in holiness and honor" (4:3).

In essence, the early church held that sex was to be reserved for marriage. At the same time, it also allowed for no marriage at all. Celibacy was an oddball counter-cultural trait of the early church. Greco-Roman and Jewish law both essentially required marriage and procreation. Thus, Paul's advocacy

---

[4] Kyle Harper, "*Porneia*: The Making of a Christian Sexual Norm" in *Journal of Biblical Literature* 131 (2012): 363–383.

for celibacy was quite liberating. Within Christianity a woman could now choose not to marry or have children and instead serve in ministry full-time. Likewise, a man could also choose a different vocation. Of course, Paul's emphasis on celibacy was motivated, in part, by the expectation that Jesus would return in the lifetime of his audience. And, he also acknowledged that celibacy is not feasible for everyone (1 Cor 7:9).

Evolving Sexual Ethics in the Bible

As we can see, sexual ethics evolved in the Jewish community. By the time of Jesus and Paul, marital and sexual monogamy were increasingly expected for Jewish men as it already was for women. Why the initial double standard and why the change? Exploring the evolution of sexual ethics in the Bible will help us see how certain ethics developed in the first place.

Why the Sexual Double Standard in the Old Testament?

The Israelites were not unique in their sexual ethics. Women's sexuality has been restricted in most cultures throughout history into modern times. One primary reason is verification of paternity for passing down inheritance through paternal bloodlines. Men want to know who their kids are. Certainty of paternity was also important for legacy. It was believed that a man achieved a kind of immortality through his progeny. His name lived on through his offspring. Even if a man died before having children, the Israelite practice of levirate marriage (the dead man's brother marrying the widow) ensured that his name would not be "blotted out of Israel" (Deut 25:5–6).

The more restrictive sexual expectations for women also appear to stem from a sense of male ownership of women.[5] As a result, premarital sex affected a woman's value in a negative way not experienced by men even if no pregnancy resulted. We can see how female virginity was prized as a type of male possession by looking at cases of rape. Tamar begs her rapist to marry her since abandonment after taking her virginity was considered worse than the rape (2 Sam 13). The rapist took something that "belonged" to a prospective husband, making other marital prospects difficult, if not impossible. The tearing of the hymen was like opening a package (Deut 22:13–21). You open it, you buy it (they seemed unaware that not all women have a hymen that tears). In contrast, male virginity was not perceived as belonging to a prospective wife.

A rapist marrying the victim was codified as an option in Israelite law (Deut 22:28–29). The law had a good intent: to hold the rapist accountable. But the willingness to give a girl to an abuser indicates the sex act affected her value and standing. It was shameful for a girl to be penetrated outside of marriage and shameful to her family. In fact, we don't need to speculate as to the rationales of rapist-victim marriage because it has continued across cultures through the modern era, even in America.[6]

---

[5] Male ownership of women is indicated in various ways in the Old Testament. For example, the Ten Commandments tell *men* not to covet what belongs to their male neighbors, listing wives alongside slaves, donkeys, and a house (Exod 20:17). Slave women were obviously owned in the technical sense, but even free women—wives and daughters—did not have autonomy. The only women who had some freedom were prostitutes or widows with enough money to survive without a man.

[6] Nicholas Kristof, "An American 13-Year-Old, Pregnant and Married to Her Rapist," *New York Times* (June 2018),

Today the double standard for women's virginity is still seen in conservative Christian purity culture. Even though boys are counseled against premarital sex, rituals are more pronounced for girls (e.g. purity rings, purity balls with one's father).[7] A quote from the ancient Jewish text Sirach could describe many conservative Christian fathers today:

> A daughter is a secret anxiety to her father, and worry over her robs him of sleep; when she is young, for fear she may not marry, or if married, for fear she may be disliked; while a virgin, for fear she may be seduced and become pregnant in her father's house (42:9–10).

Key point: The Old Testament writers didn't view male non-marital sex or multiple partners as sinful. This does not mean they supported indiscriminate promiscuity. No dating culture existed back then. Every respectable man married. A man's sexual activity generally occurred within his household, whether with wives, concubines, or slaves. Fertility was one factor in these arrangements. For example, if a wife was infertile, a slave might be used to obtain offspring.

When non-marital sex *was* considered sinful, it involved:

- a man taking a woman already betrothed or married to

---

https://www.nytimes.com/2018/06/01/opinion/sunday/child-marriage-delaware.html. See also Massoud Hayoun, "Moroccan Teen, Forced to Marry Her Rapist, Commits Suicide," *Aljazreea* (Nov 2013), http://america.aljazeera.com/articles/2013/11/22/moroccan-teen-marriedtoherrapistcommitssuicide.html

[7] Gina Dalfonzo, "Daddy Dearest: How Purity Culture Can Turn Fathers into Idols," *Christianity Today* (May 2014), https://www.christianitytoday.com/women/2014/may/daddy-dearest-how-purity-culture-turns-fathers-into-idols.html

another man (i.e. it was not sin to have extra-marital relations. with a woman who was not attached to male authority).

• confusion about a child's paternity, threatening patrimonial lines and economic stability (inheritance).

• sex only for pleasure. (This is implied; prostitution is not legally banned in the Old Testament, but frowned upon. And in the New Testament prostitution is prohibited.)

• a woman asserting personal autonomy. As with most women in the ancient Near East, Israelite women did not have equal status with men. A woman's sexuality was not her own. It belonged first to her father while a virgin and then transferred to a husband.

Male Marital & Sexual Monogamy in the New Testament

By the 3rd century BCE, the sexual double standard was disappearing. Jewish male sexuality became increasingly restricted. The shift occurred prior to the advent of Jesus, Paul, and the writings of the New Testament. What led to a change in expectations for male Jewish sexuality?

It was a reaction to Greco-Roman culture. The Greeks introduced marital monogamy to the ancient Near East.[8] At this time polygyny became a topic of debate with some Jews

---

[8] Some conservative commentators claim that monogamy was already the norm in Israelite culture and downplay evidence of polygyny. But polygyny was accepted and codified in biblical texts professed to come straight from God at Sinai (e.g. Exod 21:10; Deut 21:15–17). The only time polygyny is prohibited is for political purposes; the law banned kings from collecting numerous wives given as treaty tokens from other nations, lest leaders be led astray by the women's foreign religion (Deut 17:17).

arguing strongly against and other Jews apparently still practicing it into the 1st century CE and beyond.[9] It's not clear when the Jewish community as a whole ceased polygyny. But under Greco-Roman rule, we see new arguments against the practice, including in the Dead Sea Scrolls (based on Noah's ark and the animals entering "two by two"; *Damascus Document* 5:1-2; see also 4:20–21).

While no explicit condemnation of polygyny appears in the New Testament, Jesus and Paul refer to "two" people when referencing marriage (Mark 10:8; Eph 5:31; notably "two" is not in the Hebrew version of Genesis; these quotes draw from the Greek translation, which may have added "two" as an anti-polygyny gloss).[10] When Paul refers to spouses, he uses the singular (i.e. "wife" or "husband"). Moreover, leaders in the early church had to be the husband of one woman (1 Tim 3:2, 12; Titus 1:6; this might refer to divorce, but either way is applicable). Thus, the New Testament writers appear to have sided with Jews who affirmed marital monogamy.

Subsequently, marital monogamy likely influenced the push toward male *sexual* monogamy. The social environment for Jews changed after losing their nationhood in the 6th century BCE. They could no longer rule their own country and control their environment in the same way. Their subjection to Greeks, in particular, seemed to have a significant impact. Jews existed in the middle of a broader Hellenistic culture that

---

[9] Adiel Schremer, "How Much Jewish Polygyny In Roman Palestine?' in *Proceedings of the American Academy for Jewish Research* 63 (1997–2001): 181–223. Some early rabbinic writings discuss circumstances when a polygynous marriage might occur, suggesting polygyny continued into the 1st century and beyond for some Jews (e.g. tYev 8:5; mYev 6:5).

[10] David Instone-Brewer, *Divorce and Remarriage in the Bible: The Social and Literary Context* (Grand Rapids: Eerdmans, 2002) 61, 137.

promoted contrary customs and considerable pressure to assimilate.

Numerous opportunities existed for men to have sexual affairs in Greco-Roman culture. This naturally led to worries that Jewish men stay connected to their community by marrying Jewish girls and avoiding entanglements with non-Jewish girls. Sex with outsiders threatened cohesion in the Jewish community as most of the women available for non-marital sex were non-Jews.

We see this type of concern articulated in the ancient Jewish commentary Jubilees 25 (c. 2nd cent. BCE). Rebecca tells her son Jacob not to marry a foreign woman to ensure that his "children shall be a righteous generation and a holy seed." Jacob replies by affirming his chastity:

> I neither know nor have I touched any woman, nor have I betrothed myself to any, nor even think of taking me a wife of the daughters of Canaan. For I remember, mother, the words of Abraham, our father, for he commanded me not to take a wife of the daughters of Canaan . . . [F]or this reason I have guarded myself in my spirit against sinning or being corrupted in all my ways throughout all the days of my life; for with regard to lust and fornication, Abraham, my father, gave me many commands.[11]

Jews were disturbed by male Greco-Roman licentiousness. While the ancient Israelites allowed men to have non-marital sex, those arrangements were typically within the household. In contrast, Greco-Roman sexual practices included non-household relationships purely for pleasure. The pursuit of

---

[11] Translation from R.H. Charles, *The Apocrypha and Pseudepigrapha of the Old Testament* (Oxford: Clarendon Press, 1913), http://www.pseudepigrapha.com/jubilees/25.htm

sex for indiscriminate pleasure was appalling to Jews (and some Greco-Roman thinkers as well). Some Jews reacted by going to the other extreme and suggested that even sex for pleasure in marriage can be a problem; sex should be for procreation (Philo and Josephus; although Philo does affirm couples past child-bearing age having sex).

In his commentary on the Genesis story of Joseph, Philo attributes the seductive behavior of Pharaoh's wife to the inability "to restrain the violence of her frenzy and passion" (*On Joseph* 9 [40]). In contrast he praises Joseph's response:

> But [Joseph], proving more powerful than even the alluring opportunity, uttered a cry becoming a free man, and worthy of his race, saying, What are you forcing me to? We, the descendants of the Hebrews, are guided by special customs and laws of our own; in other nations the youths are permitted, after they are fourteen years of age, to use concubines and prostitutes, and women who make gain by their persons, without restraint. But among us a harlot is not allowed even to live, but death is appointed as a punishment for anyone who adopts such a way of life. Therefore, before our lawful marriage we know nothing of any connection with any other woman, but without ever having experienced any similar cohabitation, we approach our virgin brides as pure as themselves, proposing as the end of our marriage not pleasure but the offspring of legitimate children.[12]

Neither Jesus nor Paul suggested marital sex should only be for procreation. But by the 1st century CE Jews and

---

[12] Translation from Charles Duke Yonge, *The Works of Philo Judaeus* (London: H. G. Bohn, 1854-1890), http://www.earlychristianwritings.com/yonge/book23.html

Christians had an umbrella term, *porneia,* that was used to designate all non-marital sex as sin (although sex with slaves is not clearly addressed).[13]

Key point: Sexual ethics evolve in the Bible for men, prompted by socio-cultural dynamics. By the 3rd century BCE, Jewish male sexuality was increasingly exclusive, similarly to Jewish and Greco-Roman women. The move away from Israelite polygyny was largely influenced by Greco-Roman expectations of *marital* monogamy. It was not the result of special divine revelation unique to early Jews and Christians.

However, the shift toward male *sexual* exclusivity was a rejection of Greco-Roman licentiousness that encouraged affairs on the side. With Israel no longer an autonomous nation, there was concern that Jewish men living under Greco-Roman occupation would be tempted by foreign women and abandon their religion. The Jewish community also rejected the pursuit of sex purely for pleasure, viewing the purpose of sex as intertwined with procreation. For Paul exclusive marital sex was also a protection against promiscuity.

---

[13] Kyle Harper, "*Porneia,*" 363–383. The only possible exception is sex with a slave. *Porneia* is not really used in reference to slaves. Sex with a slave is rejected in the Jewish text Sirach 41:22a. But a contradiction is present in existing manuscripts. A Hebrew manuscript says a man should not meddle with *his own* slaves, while the Greek translation implies a man should not meddle with *his neighbor's* slaves (a violation of property). This could reflect debate in the Jewish community on the matter. Paul does not address sexual slavery, but by telling slaves to submit to their masters, he leaves open the possibility of sexual submission. That was not an uncommon use of slaves, female or male. For more on this discussion read Jennifer A. Glancy "The Sexual Use of Slaves: A Response to Kyle Harper on Jewish and Christian *Porneia*" in *Journal of Biblical Literature* 134 (2015): 215–229.

2

Bible Verses on Same-Sex Relations: A Quick Guide

Only a handful of verses in the Bible discuss same-sex relations, but they are the source of much debate as churches wrestle with how these texts inform ethics on same-sex relationships today. The following discussion provides an accessible guide to both explicit and implicit references in Scripture, as well as an analysis on their applicability.

Verses that *Explicitly* Refer to Same-Sex Relations

1. Genesis 19:1–11; Judges 19:22–25 (see also Genesis 9:20–24[14])

Traditionalist Argument: The biblical authors use homoerotic portrayals in the stories of Sodom and Gomorrah, the Levite and concubine, and Ham's offense against his father to put an exclamation point on the overall wickedness of people, whether Canaanites (Ham is the father of Canaan), Sodomites, or Benjaminites. In other words, these people weren't

[14] It is not clear if this is a case of same-sex rape or voyeurism. Some have also proposed the possibility that uncovering his father's nakedness is a reference to sex with his mother.

just wicked, they were *that* wicked.

Progressive Argument: All three of these stories refer to sexual assault. Using rape to argue against consensual, monogamous same-sex relationships makes as much sense as using the rape of the concubine in Judges 19 to argue against heterosexual marriage. In antiquity, as is often the case today, male same-sex rape was grievous because it humiliated a man by stripping him of power.

2. Leviticus 18:22 and 20:13

Traditionalist Argument: These laws refer to any type of same-sex intercourse, not just exploitative. Some have suggested they refer to temple prostitution, but the context does not state that. Also, little evidence exists for temple prostitution in the ancient Near East or Israel. Both the active and passive partner are sentenced to death, suggesting the relationship is consensual. Significantly, these laws are next to laws prohibiting incest, adultery, and bestiality—all sexual sins we still recognize as problematic today.

Progressive Argument: Deuteronomy 23:18 indicates secular homoerotic prostitution occurred, if not temple prostitution as well. That both partners are guilty in Leviticus can easily apply to prostitution as a consensual act between both parties. The author of Leviticus says the type of same-sex activity is what the *other* nations were doing, suggesting a particular form of same-sex relations.

Significantly, female same-sex relations are not prohibited in Israelite law, further suggesting the concern was not complementarity, but a culturally based form of male homoeroticism. The Levitical passage does single out women in the bestiality prohibition. Thus, the oversight for female same-sex relations cannot be attributed to a lack of concern for addressing prohibitions directly to women.

There was no concept of loving, peer same-sex marriage in the ancient Near East and Israel because marriage was highly connected to procreation and hierarchical gender norms. Moreover, many Levitical laws are no longer accepted today. The law against male same-sex relations is next to a law prohibiting sex with a menstruating woman. Leviticus also bans planting a field with two kinds of seed (19:19).

3. 1 Corinthians 6:9–10 and 1 Timothy 1:10

Traditionalist Argument: These are vice lists that include the word *arsenokoitēs*, a compound term that is adapted directly from the Greek translation of Leviticus 18:22 and 20:13 (*arsen* = "male" and *koitē* = "bed"; literally "male-bedder"). A similar, well-known Greek term is *metrokoitēs*, which refers to a person who has sex with his mother. Since Leviticus refers to non-exploitative homoeroticism, these vice lists likely imply the same. That is, any kind of same-sex activity is prohibited.

Progressive Argument: We don't know exactly what type of male-male sexual activity is indicated by the term *arsenokoitēs*. If the Levitical author had prostitution in mind, then the compound word might refer to prostitution in Paul's mind. Paul appears to have coined the term. We have no extra-biblical citations from his time period, and the vice lists provide no descriptive information. Notably, a Jewish contemporary of Paul, Philo, interpreted the Levitical prohibition as referring to pederasty and effeminate pagan temple personnel (*Special Laws* 3.37–42). In other words, Philo read Scripture in light of the kind of activity he observed in his time period.

Similarly, Paul likely had in mind the predominant, exploitative practices he saw around him: pederasty, prostitution, and master-slave rape. This is suggested by what appears in the vice lists next to the term *arsenokoitēs*. In 1 Timothy 1:10, *arsenokoitēs* appears next to "slave traders" suggesting sex trafficking. Similarly, later usage of the term by early Christians seems to have a connotation of economic exploitation.[15]

Paul might also have in view violation of patriarchal gender norms, a common concern about same-sex relations in antiquity. Sex was conceptualized in language of "active" and "passive." For a man to take the passive role in sex was to become feminized. In 1 Cor 6:9, *arsenokoitai* appears next to *malakoi* ("softies"), a term that included heterosexual self-indulgent men, as well as men who forsook patriarchal gender norms and acted "feminine." If the *malakoi* are passive partners in male-male sex, and the *arsenokoitai* are dominant partners, this suggests Paul based his objection to male same-sex relations, in part, on the common Roman dominant/submissive gender paradigm.

Another possibility is that the concern is economic. In the same passage, the *arsenokoitai* also appear next to "thieves," (v. 10), suggesting a possible connection with economic exploitation (e. g. sex trafficking).

4. Romans 1:27–28 (and possibly v. 26)

Traditionalist Argument: Romans 1:26–27 has Genesis 1–3 as a backdrop. The prohibition against homoeroticism is rooted in the creation ordinance that God intentionally created male and female to become one flesh. Thus, Paul's condemnation cannot be reduced to exploitative practices and, therefore, culturally relative behavior. This viewpoint is reinforced by the

---

[15] Dale B. Martin discusses this in *Sex and the Single Savior: Gender and Sexuality in Biblical Interpretation* (Louisville: Westminster John Knox, 2006), 39–42.

prohibition for women who were not part of the exploitative practices that progressives base their arguments on. In Romans 1, Paul points to homoeroticism (and other sins) as a symptom of the fall. We all have unhealthy and ungodly proclivities as a result of our fallen nature. These need to be redeemed, not indulged.

Moreover, the term "unnatural" indicates Paul had in mind violation of anatomical complementarity, which makes same-sex relations wrong on that ground alone whether or not the relationship is loving.

Progressive Argument: Romans 1 makes no reference to the fall in Genesis 3. Rather, Paul is writing about unbelieving Gentiles. He assumed same-sex attraction is caused by rejecting God, an assertion we know is not scientifically accurate. The primary issue in Romans 1 is idolatry, and the terminology is likely drawn from Deuteronomy 4:16–18 rather than Genesis (compare with Rom 1:22–23). Paul also engages with Wisdom of Solomon (13–14).

Paul was writing in the context of what he saw around him, namely, a type of homoeroticism rooted in pederasty, prostitution, master-slave rape, and patriarchal gender norms. He was right to denounce those things that signified people's lack of reverence for God. But these manifestations are completely different from a consensual, monogamous marriage between a same-sex couple, as advocated today.

Significantly, Romans 1:26 is the only possible place in the Bible that refers to female same-sex relations. But even this is not certain. The text does not specify *with whom* the women exchanged the natural for the unnatural. It doesn't specifically say women were having sex with other women. Some early church fathers, including Augustine thought Romans 1:26 referred to women having anal sex with men (likely as birth control).

In common Greco-Roman and Jewish usage, the term "unnatural" often referred to sex that was non-procreative or violated the dominant/submissive paradigm for gender norms. We don't have clear evidence that the objection to same-sex relations was violation of anatomical complementarity *only by itself.*

Verses that *Might Implicitly* Refer to Same-Sex Relations

1. Jude 1:6–7

Jude 1:7 indicates those in Sodom and Gomorrah were guilty of sexual immorality because they went after "strange flesh" (NASB). Some believe this is a reference to the men of Sodom who sought to rape Lot's male guests and, therefore, alludes to homoeroticism. In favor of this view, 1st century Jewish interpreters such as Philo and Josephus readily interpreted Sodom and Gomorrah as guilty of homoeroticism; but importantly they understood it as pederasty and heterosexual males with excessive, uncontrolled lust.

On the other hand, the language of "strange flesh" could be a reference to Lot's angelic guests. If "just as" is meant to connect verse 7 with verse 6, it suggests the offense was akin to angels leaving their proper abode to mate with human beings (an allusion to Genesis 6:1–7). In this case, the sexual immorality would be human/angel sexual intercourse.[16]

---

[16] Some also suggest that 2 Peter 2:4–10 might refer to homoeroticism because it has literary dependence on Jude and refers to the "lascivious" sins of Sodom and Gomorrah. However, the text does not explicitly refer to same-sex relations. If 2 Peter does have dependence on Jude, the author could be thinking of human/angel sexual intercourse.

2. Deuteronomy 23:17–18

These verses read as follows:
17: "None of the daughters of Israel shall be a *qědeshah;* none of the sons of Israel shall be a *qadesh.*
18: You shall not bring the fee of a *zonah* (female prostitute) or the wages of a *keleb* (dog) into the house of the Lord your God in payment for any vow, for both of these are abhorrent to the Lord your God."

Some interpreters believe these verses refer to male temple prostitution. In verse 18, "dog" appears to be a euphemism for same-sex prostitution. However, this might refer to ordinary prostitution rather than temple prostitution. No connotation of *religious* prostitution is present in verse 18. The interpretation is made by association to verse 17. The *qědeshah* (female) and *qadesh* (male) were temple personnel.

However, studies of these terms, *qědeshah* and *qadesh,* including their cognates in other ancient Near Eastern languages have not provided sufficient evidence that these temple jobs were sexual in nature. In that case, Deuteronomy 23 does not refer to temple prostitution. Instead what the text presents are two distinct laws. The first one forbids pagan temple personnel. The second law prohibits ordinary prostitution. Deuteronomy 23 is a list of many different types of laws back to back. Thus, the laws don't have to be associated simply by being placed together.

One could argue the two laws are placed near each other not because of prostitution, but rather idolatrous worship practices (e.g. paying vows with dirty money). That leaves the question of how "dog" should be understood. Was a "dog" a male who engaged in homoerotic activity? The parallel within the same verse with the common female prostitute (*zonah*) suggests that ordinary (and not temple) male prostitution is in view.

3. I Kings 14:24; 15:12; 22:46; 2 Kings 23:7 (see also Job 36:14)

All of these verses refer to the *qadesh*. Some have interpreted this term as referring to a male temple prostitute (and it's often translated that way in English Bibles). However, that is speculative. Studies of this term and its cognates in other ancient Near Eastern languages indicate the term refers to temple personnel but not necessarily sexual activity. The verses in Kings (and Job) do not mention any sexual activity. They don't tell us what this temple job involved except that it was associated with idolatry.

So where did the interpretation of a sexual connotation come from? The argument is based on parallels with *qĕdeshah*. The term *qĕdeshah* is used in conjunction with *zonah* in Genesis 38 (vv. 15, 21–22) and Hosea 4:14 (see also Deut 23:17–18).

A *zonah* is an ordinary female prostitute so using it together with *qĕdeshah* suggests the *qĕdeshah* is also functioning as a prostitute. However, the question is whether these parallels are synonymous. Possibly, two different types of women and activity are indicated: a common prostitute depicted alongside a pagan female temple worker (who is not a prostitute).

The other question is whether we can assume the existence of female temple prostitutes necessarily demands the existence of male temple prostitutes. That the *qĕdeshah* and *qadesh* were both temple personnel does not mean they were doing the same type of job. Female prostitution is well attested in the Hebrew Bible; male prostitution is not.

4. Mark 7:17–23 (see also Matthew 15:10–20) and Matthew 19:1–12[17]

Hypothetically, Jesus could have implicitly referred to homoeroticism. After rebuking the Pharisees for superficial purity (washing hands), he explained to his disciples that what defiles a person is immorality that comes from within (Mark 7). Among the list of vices, Jesus says *porneia* defiles a person. By the 1st century, in the Jewish community, this word had come to mean sexual immorality of all types, including that found in Leviticus 18. Homoeroticism is attested among the usage of *porneia*.[18]

However, literary references to *porneia* in ancient texts in relation to same-sex activity are few, so it is difficult to be dogmatic. We can't say for sure what Jesus envisioned when using the term given its broad and non-specific meaning of sexual immorality. Even if homoeroticism was included, what type of same-sex relations? It can refer to the common exploitative practices of the time. In fact, some scholars believe Jesus refers to and condemns pederasty (Mark 9:42).

In Matthew 19, Jesus acknowledges men with some kind of sexual difference, namely, eunuchs "from birth" (v. 12). He presumes such men do not marry because of an inability to procreate. Some have suggested eunuchs in antiquity were men who desired sex with men. But it appears some eunuchs, likely castrated as slaves, were used by women to avoid procreation.[19] In terms of eunuchs "from birth," the descriptor

---

[17] In addition, some scholars suggest that Jesus may have referred to pederasty in Mark 9:42.

[18] E.g. *Testament of Benjamin* 9:1; *Sibylline Oracles* III. 750–764; IV. 33–40. See also *porneia* in Matthew 5:32 and 19:9, as well as Acts 15:28–29 (Gentile inclusion involves abstaining from *porneia*).

[19] Juvenal, *Satura* 6.366–378 (one should also consider that Juvenal is a satirist).

suggests a visible abnormality that allowed such a diagnosis to be made at that time (i.e. intersex or other malformation).

Notably, Jesus says marriage is no longer necessary at the end of time because there will no longer be death (Luke 20:34–36). In other words, procreation is not necessary because immortality will perpetuate life instead. In antiquity, for both Greco-Romans and Jews, marriage was tightly connected to procreation. Thus, the assumption that eunuchs (and presumably other known infertile people) aren't candidates for marriage. However, Paul encourages marriage as a way to channel passions, regardless of procreation (1 Cor 7:9). For Paul, marriage is an institution that helps protect against promiscuity.

5. Revelation 22:15

This verse refers to "dogs" (*kyōn*) that are left outside the Kingdom of God at the end of the age. If an association is made with the "dog" in Deuteronomy 23:18, it could refer to male prostitutes. However, in the New Testament, this term has a broader meaning designating evil doers in general.

Bottom Line of the Debate

Both traditionalist and progressive scholars agree that the biblical authors condemned male (and possibly female) same-sex relations. The debate concerns the reasons *why* they condemned them and whether those reasons are still valid today. Significantly, the heart of the debate does not rest on the standard biblical prohibition verses. Why not? The references are too few and inconclusive for either traditionalists or progressives to dogmatically assert why same-sex relations were condemned.

One can legitimately assert that the biblical authors had exploitative practices in mind and only refer to male-male sex. We know that most same-sex relations at the time were exploitative, and we cannot prove that Romans 1 includes women. On the other hand, traditionalists can reasonably assert that the Levitical author and Paul had a permanent creation order in mind. But at the end of the day, traditionalists can't *prove* it. Neither side can prove their case.

This is why traditionalists heavily rely on Genesis 1–2 and the concept of sexual complementarity to make their case, more so than the prohibition passages. Traditionalists say the prohibition is still valid because they interpret the Genesis narratives as a mandate for heterosexual marriage, rooted in creation itself and not subject to cultural changes.

On the other hand, progressives interpret Genesis as a blessing and norm, but not a mandate. The creation stories are descriptive of the norm not prescriptive. Importantly, Genesis 1–2 does not refer to intersex people or people affected by atypical sexual development. It simply doesn't address the issue or tell us how to respond. The biblical authors had prescientific views, as evident by their understanding of cosmology. In the same way it's reasonable to consider they had prescientific views on sexual development.

The heart of the matter in the debate also comes down to how ethics should be appropriated from Scripture. For example, the biblical authors frequently engaged in a deliberative process concerning mandates that took into consideration the situation at hand, rather than blindly applying law, especially when compassion called for it.[20]

---

[20] For more on this point, see chapters 4–6 in Keen, *Scripture, Ethics, and the Possibility of Same-Sex Relationships.*

General Tips for Studying Same-Sex Relations and the Bible

1. *Use correct terminology.* "Homosexuality," "homosexual," "gay," "lesbian," or "queer" are modern terms that refer to a certain type of same-sex relations that is not necessarily the same as what was practiced in antiquity (e.g. pederasty). Modern terms have psychological or identity connotations that were not present in ancient Israel or the Greco-Roman period. Correct terminology in reference to the Bible and its historical context include: "homoeroticism," "male-male sexual intercourse," "female-female sexual intercourse," or "pederasty" (if context suggests that specifically). Same-sex "relations" but *not* "relationship" is also appropriate. The term "relationship" implies consensual, peer interactions that were not common for same-sex activity in antiquity.

2. *Distinguish between historical context and later interpretations in Christian tradition.* Understanding the historical context and the socio-cultural world of the biblical authors is important for understanding their intended meaning. Once we have done that first step, we might consider how Christian and Jewish traditions up through modern times have *interpreted* what these authors have written. Some interpretations are reasonable, but others are unhelpful innovations. One should at least be able to distinguish between historical context and later tradition, as well as when arguments are being propelled by either one or the other.

Both traditionalists and progressives engage in anachronistic interpretations in the same-sex marriage debate. That is, interpretations that project modern ideas onto the Bible that depart from the contexts of the biblical authors. For example, traditionalists paint a uniform portrait of marriage across the biblical canon. In reality, marriage took different forms (e.g.

polygyny). On the progressive side, some suggest Ruth and Naomi or David and Jonathan had a same-sex relationship. But such a conclusion is divorced from the historical realities of the biblical authors and what we know about homoeroticism in antiquity.

This is not to say creative interpretations from traditions of faith communities across time have no value. They can be integral in many respects to the life of the Church. But it becomes a problem when authoritative claims are made about "what the Bible says" that put words in the biblical authors' mouths that aren't necessarily there.

3

Hermeneutical Principles 1

1. Our social location impacts the *angle* in which we view and interpret scripture.

Social location includes where we are born and raised, the traditions we are taught, our race, gender, socio-economic status, and other factors that affect how we experience and perceive reality. For example, some African Christians are less troubled by polygamy than Western Christians, noting that the Old Testament sanctions it and the New Testament doesn't explicitly condemn it. In the Gospels we see the Pharisees viewed Sabbath from the angle of their occupation as law keepers, affecting their response to the disciples who were picking grain on the Sabbath (Mark 2:23–26; see also Exod 16:22–30; 34:21). The Pharisees had a more advantageous socio-economic status than the disciples who were traveling and did not know where their next meal was coming from.

Reflection: *How has my background shaped what I notice and don't notice in the Bible? How has my tradition taught me to read and interpret the Bible? Is it possible I have blind spots?*

2. Specific topical and word studies can be helpful but have certain limitations for ethical application.

The answer to a theological or ethical question might come from a different vantage point than one offered only by a word study. In other words, it can be an unnecessarily narrow way of exploring and evaluating an issue. Jesus did not use a Bible verse about Sabbath to address the Pharisees' concern that the disciples were violating the Sabbath by picking grain. He used a verse that applied to the situation from a different angle, namely, the *experience* of hunger, while still addressing the issue of law-breaking *generally* (Mark 2:25–28; see also Lev 24:5–9; 1 Sam 21:1–6).

Reflection: *If I want to find out what the Bible teaches about an issue, how do I normally approach the text? Do I primarily rely on word studies? What can I learn from Jesus's example of interpretation as a method to glean wisdom from Scripture?*

3. Proof-texting leads to misinterpretation.

Proof-texting is pulling one or two verses out of context to make an argument while ignoring or downplaying other verses. One example of this is pointing to a few verses in Genesis and the New Testament to suggest the Bible speaks with one voice on the topic of marriage (i.e. monogamous, one man/one woman marriage). But other verses indicate polygyny was acceptable to the writers of the Old Testament. In fact, there is good reason to believe the writer(s) of Genesis 1–2 did not object to polygyny, given its acceptance in ancient Israel. While Jesus and Paul use a Greek translation of Genesis that says the "two" shall become one flesh, the Hebrew does not have the word "two" (see Gen 2:24; Matt 19:5; Mark 10:8; Eph 5:31). The Greek translation may have incorporated "two" as a result of Greek influence toward marital monogamy. If you look up Genesis 2:24 in your Bible, which is based on the Hebrew, "two" is not there.

Reflection: *In what ways have I engaged in proof-texting? What influences me to do that? Am I afraid to acknowledge verses or passages that contradict my preferred interpretation?*

4. Flat reading leads to misinterpretation.

This involves compressing multiple texts from different books together as if they were written in one time period without attending to historical contexts. In the process we miss different biblical authors' distinct viewpoints. For example, the Bible exhibits an evolution in sexual ethics for men that occurred across time, becoming more restrictive for males. Acceptance of polygyny gave way to greater affirmation of monogamy. Changes occurred on other theological issues as well. For example, the Old Testament does not have a concept of hell; everyone good or bad goes to the same neutral place to sleep called *Sheol*. The concept of hell began to develop later during the Greco-Roman period as Jews placed their hope for justice in the afterlife.

Reflection: *In what ways have I engaged in flat reading of the Bible? What tools or educational opportunities might help me better understand the socio-historical setting of the Bible so that I can see the contextual nuances?*

5. The biblical authors did not always view outside culture as a bad influence.

While the biblical authors have plenty of negative things to say about the surrounding nations, they also borrowed what they found useful. The Israelite temple had the same three-room layout common to Phoenicians. Sacrificial practices were similar to pre-existing customs of other nations. Some proverbs have been borrowed directly from the Egyptians (see Prov 22:17–24:22 and *Teaching of Amenemope*). Jews also were receptive to Greek marital monogamy. While early rabbinic writings suggest polygyny continued among some Jews into the 1st century CE and beyond, we see Jewish writings begin actively condemning it around the 3rd and 2nd BCE after the Greeks conquered the ancient Near East.

Reflection: *What has my tradition taught me about culture, including scientific advancements? Do I believe secular culture or other religions have anything positive to offer me as a Christian? Why or why not?*

6. Paying attention to literary context is essential for correctly interpreting a particular verse or passage.

The Sodom and Gomorrah story (Gen 19) cannot be understood apart from the narrative patterns in the previous chapters. The early chapters of Genesis repeat the theme of two separate lines, the righteous line and the unrighteous line (e.g. Abel vs. Cain, Shem vs. Ham). Israel is portrayed as descending from the righteous line, while other nations are depicted as descending from the unrighteous line. The Sodom story continues this pattern contrasting Abraham with other peoples. Similarly, paying attention to what happens right before the Sodom story in chapter 18 helps us to see the antithetical parallels, especially, Abraham's hospitality contrasted with the Sodomites' inhospitality to the messengers, which symbolizes their degree of openness to hear from God.

Reflection: *When I read a verse, do I have a habit of studying the content that goes before and after? Do I read a whole biblical book to understand its overall theological message before trying to interpret a specific verse or passage?*

7. Reception history helps us to understand how later generations received and interpreted biblical texts.

Philo, a Jewish theologian who lived at the same time as Jesus and Paul, interpreted the Sodom story and Leviticus 18 as referring to pederasty (men having sex with boys). He also understood Leviticus through the lens of the pagan temple practices he observed in his own culture. What did the original author of Leviticus 18 mean when he was writing 500+ years earlier than Philo and Paul the Apostle? It may have been a slightly different nuance, possibly related to prostitution. It's unclear except that it was a form of homoeroticism that the biblical author said *other* nations were engaging in (Lev 18:3, 24–25, 27–28, 30). There is good reason to believe Paul interpreted Leviticus similarly to Philo, based on the most prevalent forms of same-sex relations in his cultural context (e.g. pederasty, prostitution).

Reflection: *Am I only interpreting the Bible through what Christians are saying today? How often do I read primary texts from Jews and Christians throughout history to see how they received and interpreted a passage?*

Resources for Interpretation

- Bible commentaries are helpful for understanding literary and socio-cultural context. Not all commentaries are equal. For a start, try *Interpretation: A Bible Commentary for Preaching and Teaching* and *Word Biblical Commentary.*

• Read primary texts of early church fathers' interpretations of the Bible. *Ancient Christian Commentary on Scripture* (a commentary series) is a good place to start.

• Read books on how to interpret the Bible such as *The Art of Reading Scripture* by Ellen Davis and Richard Hays and *Reading the Bible with the Dead: What You can Learn from the History of Exegesis that You Can't Learn from Exegesis Alone* by John Thompson. Mark Noll's book is also essential for contemplating biblical interpretation: *The Civil War as a Theological Crisis.*

Part 2:
Normative Ethics

Applying Scriptural principles of
sexual ethics for Christian life and practice today.

4

What Does the Bible Say about Sex? Wisdom for Today

Does the Bible have divine wisdom to offer us on sexual relationships today? Or do the viewpoints of ancient Israelites and early Jews and Christians reflect ethics shaped by their socio-cultural context? On one hand, it would be cross-culturally arrogant to think we have all the answers and nothing to learn from another people group. Yet, on the other hand, the cultural distance is evident, at least in the West. Some practices that made sense to them in their context are not ethics we should follow (e.g. rapist-victim marriage to hold a rapist accountable; Deut 22:28–29; see also 2 Sam 13). Can we trust Scripture to offer divinely inspired and enduring truths on sexual ethics? In this essay, I explore why I believe we can.

To say Scripture gives us a divinely inspired Christian sexual ethic does not mean we affirm all the ethical perspectives of the biblical authors. It is important to distinguish between *descriptive* ethics and *normative* ethics. Descriptive ethics are the morals of ancient Jews and Christians that reflect their socio-cultural context. Normative ethics are how we draw principles from Scripture for morality today. The question is: how do we determine if there should be continuity or discontinuity between the ethics of the biblical authors and Christians today?

Two primary interpretive approaches can guide us. First, we look for the moral logic behind the biblical authors' sexual ethics to determine enduring principles. Some dismiss the biblical authors as holding a confusing array of sexual ethics (e.g. different types of marriages) and, therefore, the Bible has little clear guidance on sexuality. But this conclusion often stems from ignorance of socio-cultural context; the biblical authors' sexual ethics were coherent to them at the time. There was a rhyme and reason, even for rapist-victim marriage, that usually pertained to communal stability and well-being.[21]

Second, we look for patterns across the scriptural canon. Proof-texting one verse to create a theology on sex is liable to result in erroneous conclusions. In contrast, enduring ethics are likely to show up repeatedly across the Old and New Testaments. The following discussion examines the moral logic and canonical patterns on sexuality in Scripture to propose a normative Christian ethic.

Sex Is Connected to Community Wellbeing

The biblical authors viewed sex in the context of community stability. It was not considered an individualistic pursuit. Sex is related to social wellness. Historically, most communities develop sexual ethics that are in some way beneficial to the whole. An obvious example is the prohibition against adultery, which is common across cultures. Adultery violently disrupts the cohesion and harmony of a family unit. While adultery has sometimes been defined differently for men, the

---

[21] See chapter 4 in Karen R. Keen, *Scripture, Ethics, and the Possibility of Same-Sex Relationships* for more on the cultural context of Israelite laws, including the rapist-victim marriage law.

New Testament holds men to the same standards as women.[22] Philo, a 1st century Jewish theologian, lamented that adultery destroys family and makes "vain the hopes which men conceive of having legitimate children" (*Special Laws* 3.11).[23]

Sometimes the objections biblical authors had to non-marital sex were gender-specific because of distinct social effects. For women, a primary concern was out-of-wedlock pregnancy. For men, it was temptations to apostasy. Both of these concerns were primarily about social stability. Ancient Jews were concerned that out-of-wedlock pregnancy diminished a woman's chances of marriage, as well as placed a child in limbo, preventing full integration as a proper descendant. Both involved economic concerns. A father might not have the ability to provide for a daughter who never married. Similarly, a child who was unable to prove paternity fell outside the lines of patrimonial inheritance, making survival more difficult.

Concerns for social stability also encouraged Jewish male sexual exclusivity in the Greco-Roman period. Ancient Jews were worried their men might become entangled with non-Jewish women. That, in turn, affected the social stability of the community. Survival of the community depended on sons remaining faithful and invested. Similarly, Paul urges Christians not to become "unequally yoked" out of concern that it will make it more difficult for a believer to live a Christ-centered life (2 Cor 6:14–18). He also witnessed how interfaith marriages could lead to divorce when an unbelieving spouse abandoned his partner (1 Cor 7:15).

---

[22] See essay in the present volume titled, "What Does the Bible Say about Sex? A Historical Overview."

[23] Translation from Charles Duke Yonge, *The Works of Philo Judaeus* (London: H. G. Bohn, 1854–1890), http://www.earlychristianwritings.com/yonge/book29.html.

In essence, for sex to be ethical, the biblical authors believed it had to concern not only the couples' pleasure (which is valued; see Gen 18:12; Prov 5:18–19), but also community and familial cohesion. Thus, adultery, out-of-wedlock pregnancy, and interfaith marriage were troubling for the instability and disconnection they caused.

Of course, the way Jews and Christians sometimes fostered communal well-being could be problematic. In an honor-shame culture, offending parties, especially women, might be ostracized or killed (John 8:3–4). Ironically, this perpetuated another kind of community rupture.

Paul's contemplation on divorce is helpful for how Christians can uphold a value without responding punitively. Unlike his forefathers who demanded that an interfaith spouse be banished (Ezra 10:10–11, 16–17) or even killed (Num 25), Paul says to remain married to an unbelieving spouse. Only if that partner abandons the marriage should a person accept the separation/divorce. Paul counseled this even as he urged Christians, who had not married yet, to avoid becoming unequally yoked. Thus, he models a grace-filled response to a complex situation when an unequal yoke is already the present reality for a couple.

A normative Christian sexual ethic, then, will continue to ask how sexual behavior impacts community welfare as a whole, particularly as it relates to the stability of marriages and the wellbeing of children. And it will find grace-filled, not shame-based, ways to do that.

Self-Control Is a Sign of Healthy Sexuality

When the Jerusalem Council affirmed the integration of Gentiles into the Christian faith, they affirmed that God desires all people, Gentiles and Jews, to avoid sexual immorality (*porneia*; Acts 15:20, 29). Paul agreed with this decision, upholding

Jewish sexual ethics for Gentiles. Shortly after the Council agreement, Paul taught the Thessalonians that a Christian is someone who knows "how to control your own body in holiness and honor, not with lustful passion, like the Gentiles who do not know God" (1 Thess 4:3–5). He exhorted, "The fruit of the Spirit is . . . self-control" (Gal 5:22–23). Self-control is evidence that the Spirit is guiding a person's body and actions. If we live a Spirit-filled life, we will not indulge desires simply because we have them (v. 16). Paul also suggests self-control in marriage is healthy, counseling that couples might temporarily refrain for periods of prayer (1 Cor 7:5).

The concern was not that sex is bad. The biblical authors affirm sex is good. It was later Christians who began to view sexual desire as the result of the fall, departing from the biblical authors' views. Rather the concern for self-control was not only its importance for community well-being (e.g. danger of passion fueled adultery), but also the Christian belief that we are more than the sum of our appetites. Sexual desire like other appetites is to be engaged with moderation (e.g. 1 Cor 6:12–13; Phil 3:18–19).

This is why many religions, including Christianity, have noted the benefits of fasting for learning moderation. Fasting trains the body to submit to the Spirit, sitting patiently with the discomfort of delayed gratification. That training enables a person to resist the powerful physical urges to commit adultery or to overeat while others go hungry. Importantly, self-control is different than asceticism, which punishes the body for its desires, flogging and starving it. To the contrary, the body is good, and its best Self shines when it surrenders to the Spirit's wisdom.

The Spirit guides the body to readily give itself to acts of selflessness, which often involve delayed gratification. Lack of self-control makes it more likely to act out of selfish ambition. For example, the biblical authors viewed gluttony as a social justice issue; an overfed appetite results in some people having too much, while others do not have enough (Amos 4:1–3; Luke 16:19–31). Similarly, Paul expressed concern "that no one wrong or exploit a brother or sister" as a result of unchecked sexual desire (1Thess 4:6). Self-control is a way of practicing justice.

Yet Paul also recognizes the difficulty of sexual self-control. He doesn't counsel "don't have sex" as the solution to sexual passion, instead he advises the supportive structure of marriage. He teaches married couples to have regular sex to guard against extra-marital affairs (1 Cor 7:5) and directs single people who are unable to control themselves sexually to marry (v. 9). Marriage provides a rudder for sexual desire.

Of course, in an effort to promote and achieve the good of self-control, religious institutions can be tempted into legalism. Importantly, controlling behavior by an external force is not the same thing as *self*-control or submitting to the *Spirit's* authority. External efforts to control can become abusive and tend to disproportionally harm women.

To counter legalism, Paul counsels: "For you were called to freedom, brothers and sisters; only do not use your freedom as an opportunity for self-indulgence . . . 'You shall love your neighbor as yourself'" (Gal 5:13–14). A healthy approach to sexuality is paradoxically rooted in our freedom to choose, and Paul urges us to use that freedom for its intended purpose of caring for others. Freedom that is guided by self-sacrificial love, not rules, empowers us to resist sin.

A normative Christian sexual ethic, then, will champion self-control as a life-giving value, particularly for the way it puts other people's well-being at the forefront and not one's own gratification. And it will foster this through voluntary submission of one's desires to the Spirit, and not through legalism.

Our Bodies Belong to God for a Purpose

One unique aspect of Christianity is the priesthood of all believers (1 Pet 2:5–9; see also Exod 19:6). Not just leaders are set apart (sanctified) for God, but all Christians are set-apart *from* common use *for* divine service. Paul urged believers to offer our bodies as "living sacrifices" (Rom 12:1–2). Our bodies are not our own because we have been "bought with a price" (1 Cor 6:19–20; see also v. 13). Similarly, we are creatures handcrafted by God for a purpose. We were "created in Christ Jesus for good works, which God prepared beforehand to be our way of life" (Eph 2:10).

The biblical authors indicate any decision we make with our bodies should ask: Does this use of my body reflect my status as set apart for God's purposes? Is it a way to offer myself as a sacrifice to God? Does this action reflect the good deeds God prepared for me to do? For the biblical authors, sex could not be separated from God's greater salvific plans for humanity. Sex was to look differently for Christians than unbelievers (1 Thess 4:3–5). As one example, the Christian sexual union is related to Christ's love for the church (Eph 5:31–32).

A normative Christian sexual ethic, then, is not only about consent between two people, but also about God's overarching plan for our bodies as set-apart for Kingdom purposes. While secular humanism has many good values shared with Christian sexual ethics, ultimately, sex for the Christian is to be distinctly Christian.

Covenant Is the Best Context for Sex

By the time the New Testament was written, and before Jesus and Paul were born, Jewish sexual ethics reserved sex for marriage (for men and women). The Jerusalem Council determined that Jewish sexual ethics would be the basis for Christian sexual ethics.[24]

A primary reason for this is that the biblical authors viewed sex as connected to family and community. This was true even for the ancient Israelites when men could have more than one sexual partner. Concubines and slaves were generally part of the Israelite household and supported within the family unit, even as they were of lesser status. A primary concern with male Greco-Roman sexual practices was sex for pleasure apart from commitment. Paul counseled against hook-ups with a prostitute, saying that such an act is not congruent with a Christian use of the body (1 Cor 6:12–17). In other words, sex cannot be reduced *only* to pleasure.

This was not a prudish objection to pleasure. Rather, sex was deemed an investment in a person more holistically. Thus, Paul urges men who are tempted to have sex with their betrothed to go ahead and marry (7:6). A sexual relationship is meant to extend beyond intercourse to caring for another person's daily non-sexual needs. Since our bodies are the temple of the Holy Spirit, Paul also sees sex as bringing God into the act. Thus, the purpose of the union matters spiritually.

Genesis describes leaving one's mother and father in order to cleave to a mate (*dabaq*; Gen 2:23–24). This cleaving is the creation of a new family unit. In cleaving, a person becomes kin. For the biblical authors sex is about creating home and household. This is not to say the Israelites always practiced this. Some biblical descriptions are disturbing, particularly of women taken captive during war time and then discarded (Deut 21:10–14).

Yet, the majority of Old Testament texts portray slaves and concubines as integrated into household. And with the advent

---

[24] See the first essay in this volume, "What Does the Bible Say about Sex: A Historical Overview"

of marital monogamy in the Greco-Roman world, Jews and Christians translated that into the practice of sexual monogamy, keeping physical intimacy in the context of household.

The household was held together by marital covenant. So important was this covenant that it became a predominant metaphor that the biblical authors used to describe God's relationship with Israel and the church. The covenant that God made with Israel during her rescue from Egypt is framed as marriage (Jer 2:2; 31:31–33; See also Isa 54:5; 62:4–5; Hosea 2:16–20).

Similarly, Paul described Christ's relationship with the church in marital terms, emphasizing the deep love and caring that characterizes covenant (Eph 5:25–33). For the biblical authors, the marital covenant was the most potent imagery for capturing God's enduring faithfulness.

Perhaps the most vivid description of God's relationship with us is the Song of Songs. Throughout Jewish and Christian history the Song has been interpreted as a metaphor of God's love relationship with humanity.[25] While in more recent years it has been read as human love poetry, it was

---

[25] While it's possible the original use of Song of Songs only had human beings in mind (the origin is unknown), we do know it does not depict a dating relationship. The only girls or women available for sexual relations outside of marriage were prostitutes, slaves, or concubines. In Israelite culture, a man was not restricted to one sexual partner so portrayal of sexual relations with someone not a wife, would not be unheard of. The original meaning may be metaphorical as it has long been interpreted, but the original might also refer to a man's relationship with a concubine. The Song also appears to have allusions to Eden and could be a reflection on Genesis's Adam and Eve. In any case, by the 1st century, extra-marital sexual relations were no longer acceptable for men as the Jewish community embraced marital monogamy and sexual monogamy.

originally incorporated into the canon for its metaphorical meaning.

In fact, a dating relationship was not possible in the patricentric culture of antiquity, which closely guarded women's sexuality and married off girls shortly after puberty. But ancient writers of the Song knew what it felt like to be in love, just as we do, and could draw from that human experience to point to a transcendent reality.

In the book of Revelation, we see the ultimate marriage depicted as God dwelling in household with humanity:

> And I saw the holy city, the new Jerusalem, coming down out of heaven from God, prepared as a bride adorned for her husband. And I heard a loud voice from the throne saying, 'See, the home of God is among mortals. He will dwell with them; they will be his peoples, and God himself will be with them' (21:2–3; see also 19:7–9).

For the biblical authors, sex includes pleasure, but is much more than that—it is what creates a kinship bond and household. Yet, as with other meaningful Scriptural values for sexual ethics, such as community well-being or self-control, the good of covenant can be twisted into legalism. It can be held up in a way that shames those who are divorced, unable to find a spouse, or not virgins on their wedding day.

The blessing of covenant that God gives is not meant to be used as a weapon. Scripture reminds us that the unmarried have their rightful place (Isa 54:1), God is merciful in allowing divorce when a spouse has been harmed (Matt 5:32; I Cor 7:15), and Christ does not ostracize those caught up in sexual sin (John 4:4–42; 8:1–11).

A normative sexual ethic, then, places sexual relations in the context of life-long covenant and not casual sex. Sex involves investment in another person's daily life needs, not the fulfillment of pleasure alone. Yet, this good must be upheld without shaming those who have experienced sex outside of this context.

A Better Way Than Shame and Rules

Formulating a Christian sexual ethic naturally raises the question of shame. The problems with purity culture are real. Many of us who grew up in the church were taught that any non-marital sex made us dirty and forever tainted. There was no getting back virginity or sexual purity. Once that line was crossed, we lost something essential that could never be regained. Or so we were told.

It is no wonder the church's treatment of sex has often caused so much shame and anxiety. The problem with purity culture is that it attempts to coerce sexual wellness through fear and rules. Yet this is not a biblical approach to sexual ethics. In fact, it often leads to more dysfunction as people hide their sexual desires and activity to avoid rejection and condemnation.

Paul taught that rules are ineffective because sin actually uses rules against us: "While we were in the flesh, our sinful passions, *aroused by the Law*, were at work in our members" and "Sin, *seizing an opportunity in the commandment*, produced in me all kinds of covetousness. Apart from the law sin lies dead" (Rom 7:5, 8). In other words, the moment we say to ourselves, "Thou shall not" is the moment we add fuel to the flames.

It is not the rule itself that is bad (Rom 7:7–13). For example, if we have a tendency to overindulge a sweet tooth, not eating any more cookies might be a smart idea. Yet, sin sees rules as an exciting opportunity to break them.

Think about what happens when you see a sign that says, "Don't walk on the grass." Suddenly, walking on the grass sounds like a brilliant idea. You might not have even noticed the grass before. You might not have had any previous desire to walk on the grass. But now that you have seen that sign all you dream of are soft green blades between your toes. Or if grass is not your thing, think of a museum sign that says "Do not touch."

Psychiatrist Viktor Frankl described a similar, though not exact, concept in his theory of Logotherapy: "In the same way that fear brings to pass what one is afraid of, likewise a forced intention makes improbable what one forcibly wishes."[26] He proposes "paradoxical intention." Rather than trying *not* to do something, one is given freedom to do that very thing. In treating clients with anxiety, Frankl coached them to, deliberately, try to feel anxious.

Many of us have experienced the phenomenon of seeking to reduce our anxiety only to have it increase the more we tried to suppress it. If we used paradoxical intention, we would tell ourselves, "I'm going to try to feel as anxious as possible; I'm going to make my heart beat faster; I'm going to make myself shake nervously." Surprisingly, anxiety often subsides with paradoxical intention.

While it would not be advisable to go out and eat as many cookies as possible (or have sex in whatever context one desires), a form of paradoxical intention is exactly what Scripture says strips sin of its power. If sin has more power when we are bound to rules, what is the solution? Freedom from rules. Thus, Scripture says, "Now we have been released from the Law . . . so that we serve in newness of the Spirit" (Rom 7:6; NASB).

This, of course, does not mean we should engage in self-indulgence. Paul writes, "What then? Should we sin because

---

[26] Viktor E. Frankl, *Man's Search for Meaning* (Boston: Beacon Press, 2006), 122.

we are not under law but under grace? By no means!" (6:15). He admonishes, "For you were called to freedom, only do not turn your freedom into an opportunity for the flesh, but through love serve one another" (Gal 5:13; NASB).

The paradoxical effect of freedom makes many Christians nervous. We are, quite frankly, afraid of our freedom. We cling to rules because they give us the illusion of control. Yet, as Paul pointed out, "Why do you submit to regulations, 'Do not handle, Do not taste, Do not touch?' . . . These have indeed an appearance of wisdom . . . but they are of no value in checking self-indulgence" (Col 2:20–23).

Why are they of no value? Because the dynamic force of sin is more powerful than human strength. Relying on willpower, through the use of rules, will typically make the sin struggle even more pronounced and difficult.

We can only win the wrestling match against unwanted behavior through supernatural means. It is the "law of the *Spirit* of life in Christ Jesus" that frees us from the operating principles of sin (Rom 8:2). Freedom shifts us from relying on rules to depending on the Spirit to achieve a godly life.

How the Spirit Empowers Us to Live a Christian Sexual Ethic

Freedom strips everything to its authentic bare-bones. When we are no longer bound to rules, it leaves us at a crossroad to ponder the direction we will take. *It exposes our motives.* Instead of obeying God out of rote obligation or fear of hell, our freedom allows us to ask: What do I really want to do? And what does my decision tell me about myself and my relationship with God?

Some will use such freedom as an excuse to self-indulge and get away with as much as possible. Others will follow rules out of fear or to prove themselves "good." But those who are motivated by love (not fear) will stop at that crossroad and think, "I really want to indulge this sin. I really do. But as much as I want it, and as much as I know God's grace covers it, I love God more than I love this sin."

Our freedom allows us to express our love for God more than we ever could when bound to rules. Freedom gives us the opportunity to *choose* to love God. If we do not understand the extent of God's grace, we will never understand our freedom, and if we don't understand our freedom, we will never love God at the deepest level possible. Thus, walking by the Spirit begins first with understanding and resting in God's unbelievable grace and acceptance. Ultimately, it is not through rules that we walk by the Spirit; it is through love (Gal 5:16–25).

The more we actively pursue God in love, the more the Spirit matures us over time, breaking us free of sinful thoughts and behaviors. The love-pursuit of God is what it means to walk by the Spirit rather than rules. Walking by the Spirit is less about starting/stopping a particular behavior and more about *being*.

This way of being results when the fruit of the Spirit emanates from us. When we seek these inner spiritual attributes, they overflow to produce the outward behavior we desire. So, instead of praying, "God help me stop doing such and such," it would be more helpful to pray, "God fill me with love, truthfulness, humility, wisdom, sober-mindedness, and perseverance." Notice that these are not rules to follow, but character traits to grow in. Practically speaking, here is what that might look like:

Love

Love begins in relationship with God. We learn to love by receiving God's love (Luke 7:47; 1 John 1:19). God loves us unconditionally before we ever love God. God is not an accountant in the sky keeping a record of all our mistakes. God is a relational being who looks at us with compassion. Ultimately, receiving God's love and returning it is how we learn to walk by the Spirit.

Sometimes sex is confused for love. Understandably so, it releases bonding hormones, and our bodies are physically close and intimate with another's. But sex is not love; sex trafficking and other forms of exploitation make this fact obvious. Yet sex is to be characterized by love.

Love will not only forsake personal desires, but even life itself for the benefit of another (John 15:13). Love is patient, kind, humble, gives up one's own expectations and demands, is peaceable, forgiving, grieves at wrong doing, and clings to truth (1 Cor 13:4–7).

To distinguish between love versus a compulsion to connect with someone out of our own need or attraction, we have to examine our motives. Do our actions and words encourage others to live life fully for God? Are we willing to give up a dating relationship if God asks us to? Are we honoring that person's body and emotions? Are we doing what is in that person's best interest? Do we treat people with dignity and respect, or are we subtly manipulative and selfish?

Truthfulness

Sometimes I love sin more than God. Sin brings pleasure; that's why we do it. In the past, I didn't want to acknowledge my love for sin. It didn't seem like an effective strategy to get on God's good side. Wouldn't God be upset if I just came out and said all the sinful things I wanted to do? I didn't think that would impress God very much.

So, I played mind games with myself. I would go over to a certain friend's house to "chat" when what I really wanted was sexual intimacy. When the visit would culminate in exactly that, I would think, "What? How did that happen?" I felt less guilty believing I had "accidentally" stumbled than truthfully acknowledging I wanted, or even planned, to go against my conscience.

If we want to overcome certain problematic behavior, we need to be brutally honest with God: "Lord I'm going to the grocery store right now to buy three packages of cookies and I'm going to eat them all as soon as I get home."[27] The more we are honest the more we open the door to a heart to heart talk with God. Perhaps, we will discover the real issue is loneliness or anxiety, and God might have a better suggestion for addressing that than eating three packages of cookies (or hooking up). Or, perhaps our truthfulness will reveal that we don't trust God. Or, that our hearts are hard against God.

When I feel reluctant to do what God tells me, I pray, "Lord give me the desire to follow your ways because I really don't want to. And even if I did, I'm not sure I know how. Help me find joy in your counsel. Help me see this sin for what it is."

Humility

One of the hardest aspects of living out a godly sexual ethic is living in various stages of imperfection. Our imperfection means we will experience cognitive dissonance. We will do what we don't want to do. There will be a contradiction between our beliefs and our behavior. Cognitive dissonance can cause

---

[27] I am indebted to a former seminary professor, Dr. David Eckman, who helped me to understand God's grace and compassion amid our weaknesses such that we are free to be brutally honest with God without fear. Dr. Eckman talked about this concept in his class drawing from his curriculum called *Becoming What God Intended*.

mental health problems, including depression and anxiety. As a result, we sometimes abandon faith to fully embrace dysfunction. That is, we change our theological beliefs to match our behavior. This provides relief from the tension. But, ultimately, it doesn't get us where we need to go.

The only way we can survive cognitive dissonance is through humility. Humility means dependency on God's lavish grace and forgiveness. We must grasp the reality that God's grace is greater than any of our failures. God's grace (and the humility to accept it) is the antidote to the despair that inevitably arises with cognitive dissonance.

The fact is we are never going to be perfect in this lifetime. The next time our failures tempt us to despair, let us turn it into praise and gratitude for God's amazing mercy. Let us turn it into an opportunity to grow in humility.

Wisdom

Wisdom gives us the guidance we need to make decisions that are edifying. Wisdom keeps us from acting foolishly and impulsively. So much of overcoming sin involves making wise decisions. Scripture says the beginning of wisdom is reverence for God. God is the source of wisdom; we find it when we seek God. Scripture also says we should ask for wisdom and God will give it to us.

To be wise is to be sober-minded. Sometimes we get caught up in fantasies or become high on desires, resulting in lapses in judgment. Sober-mindedness keeps our feet grounded in reality and not fantasy or frivolous worldly things.

Do we think about the consequences of our decisions, or do we live impulsively in the moment? Are we getting as close as we can to fire without touching it, or are we fleeing temptation? When we make decisions, do we ask ourselves, "Can I 'technically' get away with it?" Or, do we ask, "Is this the wisest decision I can make? Does it do everything possible to draw me closer to God?"

Perseverance

I grew up on stories of sudden, dramatic conversions—stories of those caught in vices, who, upon reciting the Sinner's Prayer, were instantaneously delivered. There is a myth in the Church that says if we verbalize the right prayer or have enough faith, we won't struggle with unwanted behavior.

While God does, at times, empower instantaneously, this is not the norm. Spiritual growth happens over time. It requires patience and perseverance. Walking by the Spirit is like a growing tree. We don't see a tree grow in the moment. But wait a few months, a year, ten years and the sapling, eventually, becomes a solid oak.

Too often we give up when we don't see the change we want. We get tired and drop out of the race. We need God's Spirit to give us endurance to press forward. As Paul writes, "Let us run with perseverance the race that is set before us, looking to Jesus . . . who for the sake of the joy that was set before him endured the cross . . . Consider him who endured . . . that you may not grow weary or lose heart" (Heb 12:1–3).

Conclusions

Scripture provides helpful divinely inspired guidance for our sex lives. It leads us to a sexual ethic that is attentive to community well-being, self-control, set-apart bodies for God's purposes, and covenantal household. Importantly, these values only bring life when we are given freedom to choose them and not coerced by shame. The Spirit-empowered life thrives on God's grace, not rules.

5

What Is Marriage?

What motivated you to get married? Or if you are not married, what might compel you to seek that union? Across time and culture that question has been answered differently depending on circumstances and context.

My aunt Alma married at age 17 to uncle Albert during WWII because they discovered only married couples would receive land from the occupying army. Their rushed wedding was motivated by a desire to survive the war. Historically, marriage has been driven by the need for offspring to work the land and care for the elderly. Marriages have also served to benefit families economically by "marrying up."

On the other hand, when survival is not threatened, different motivations often take the lead, including desire for companionship or children for nonutilitarian purposes. Still another purpose of marriage offered by evangelical pastor Tim Keller is sanctification: Marriage "is for helping each other to become our future glory-selves, the new creations that God will eventually make us."[28]

How we understand the purpose of marriage affects whether same-sex couples might be included. For example, if marriage is for procreation, that dictates a heterosexual union.

---

[28] Tim Keller, *The Meaning of Marriage* (Penguin Books, 2013), 120.

But if marriage is for sanctification, learning to love self-sacrificially is a noble endeavor applicable to same-sex couples.

Does Including Same-Sex Couples Negatively Redefine Marriage?

In his article "In Defense of Marriage," Ryan T. Anderson argues that marriage is foundational to civilization because it relates to how children are reared.[29] Children must be raised in an optimal context to become healthy leaders of the future. He writes, "State recognition of marriage protects children by incentivizing adults to commit permanently and exclusively to each other and their children." Children should be raised by their biological mother and father to minimize societal dysfunction that stems from family disintegration.

Anderson believes if sexual complementarity is taken out of the definition of marriage it will cause men and women to be less committed to their marriages, leading to less commitment to children. Marriage will be defined by the emotional needs of adults, rather than the shared responsibility of raising children.

He argues that the inclusion of same-sex couples would foster divorce and polyamory/polygamy. In his view, no reason would exist for a couple to stick together should the emotional intensity abate, nor would any reason remain to limit marriage to two people. Taking sexual complementarity out of the equation would lead to higher rates of unwed pregnancies because heterosexuals would not see the need for gender diversity in marriage. Fathers would be optional and

---

[29] Ryan Anderson, "In Defense of Marriage," The Heritage Foundation (2013),
https://www.heritage.org/marriage-and-family/commentary/defense-marriage

men would internalize this, decreasing motivation to stay committed to their families.

Anderson is surely right that commitment and exclusivity are important for marriage and raising children, but his thesis is problematic. First, polygamy has been prominent throughout history and across cultures long before same-sex couples were included in marriage. In fact, polygamy was accepted by the authors of the Old Testament. It often occurs in cultures where family structures are patricentric and gender norms are strictly defined. Prohibiting same-sex couples from marrying will not prevent the pursuit of more than one partner. It never has.

Second, heterosexuals redefined marriage to an emotional bond long before marriage of same-sex couples was legalized. Emotional unions as a basis for marriage was written into the books through modern contraception, no-fault divorce laws, and Roe vs. Wade.[30] That ship has already sailed. The question Anderson has not asked is why *heterosexuals* initiated the separation of marriage from commitment and procreation. Anderson might also consider how factors like educational level and socio-economic status play a role in the vulnerability of family cohesion. Ironically, a legal brief written by opponents of marriage equality acknowledged these factors:

> Making marriage genderless may have little impact on those who are now married or who are well educated, well-to-do, religious and/or otherwise committed to the marital norm of sexual intercourse only between husband and wife. But *marginal* marriage candidates—including the poor, relatively uneducated, irreligious or others who

[30] I am indebted to Ron Belgau, who made this point in personal correspondence.

are highly influenced by cultural messages promoting casual and uncommitted sex—likely will be affected.[31]

Problematically, opponents of marriage equality blame gay and lesbian people for heterosexual dysfunction, rather than addressing the root issues, including poverty, educational needs, lack of spiritual formation, promiscuity, and infidelity. All of these factors pre-existed the acceptance of same-sex couples.

Is Procreation *Required* for Marriage?

Basic biology tells us that male and female are designed for procreative union. Like other animal forms, sexual dimorphism serves to perpetuate the human race. However, distinct from other animals is the institution of marriage, infused with meaning beyond procreation.

Many couples desire children and have them. A recent analysis shows that 86% of American women will have children in their lifetime (a 7.5% increase from 2006).[32] This nesting tendency is evident even for those who eschew wedlock. Despite marrying later, people are "setting up house" in cohabitating relationships at the same young age as the past.

Similarly, marriage delay is not stopping many women from having children—48% of all childbirths in the U.S. are to unmarried women and most of them are not teenagers.[33] In

---

[31] Gene C. Schaerr, et al., "Brief of Amici Curiae 100 Scholars of Marriage in Support of Respondents," (2015), 30.

[32] Belinda Luscombe, "No, All Those Strollers Aren't Your Imagination: More Women Are Having Children, *Time* (2018), https://time.com/5107704/more-women-mothers/

[33] Ezra Klein, "Nine Facts about Marriage and Childbirth in the United States," *Washington Post* (2013),

other words, desire to set up house and have children is still operating even as people try to resist it by choosing to marry later.

Biology tells us that procreation cannot be cleanly separated from marriage for heterosexual couples. Sex between males and females naturally leads to procreation. More than one million abortions in America each year testify that those who choose not to have children are still affected by the realities of reproductive organs.

Condoms, birth control, even vasectomies are not 100% guarantees in preventing conception. Technology cannot make up for the "heat of the moment," poor judgment brought on by alcohol or other means, a boyfriend who doesn't want to wear the condom, or simply forgetting to take the pill.

Thus, marriage for heterosexuals requires accepting that pregnancy is a possibility even if one does not desire it or plan for it. A 2011 study showed that 45% of all pregnancies in the U.S. are unintended.[34] While modern contraception does drastically decrease the chance of pregnancy like never before in history, the fact remains that unless one is infertile, it's impossible to guarantee that conception will never occur.

No wonder marriage has always been tied to procreation. Historically, it was *inevitable* prior to modern contraception, as well as today where contraception is not readily available. Yet even with available advanced contraception, pregnancy is still a common natural outcome.

---

http://www.washintonpost.com/blogs/wonkblog/wp/2013/03/25/nine-facts-about-marriage-and-childbirth-in-the-united-states/ (and http://onlinelibrary.wiley.com/doi/10.1111/jomf.12123/abstract)

[34] "Unintended Pregnancy," Centers for Disease Control and Prevention,
http://www.cdc.gov/reproductivehealth/unintendedpregnancy/

For heterosexuals, it's not always possible to separate sex from procreation. Thus, it often characterizes marriage by default. Add to this the fact that more than 90% of the population is heterosexual and procreation becomes the prevailing expectation of coupling, again by default. *But here is the key question: Must natural outcome mean required?*

Significantly, Anderson, in a separate co-written article with Sherif Girgis and Robert George, says it is not. He supports the marriage of infertile couples saying, "In truth marriage is not a mere means, even to the great good of procreation. It is an end in itself, worthwhile for its own sake. So, it can exist apart from children."[35] They go on to say that it would be "unfair" to exclude infertile couples from marriage.

Having admitted marriage is an end in itself apart from procreation, Anderson, Girgis, and George struggle to find a rationale to exclude same-sex couples. Ultimately, they conclude that vaginal penetration is the determining factor of whether or not a marriage is legitimate. If a relationship has not been consummated it is not a marriage. They maintain that sexual activity such as oral or anal sex does not qualify as consummation; a penis must penetrate a vagina.[36] They don't adequately address heterosexual couples who are unable to function sexually this way, for example, as a result of disability.

Yet if marriage is "worthwhile for its own sake," surely it is worthwhile for reasons far beyond the act of penile penetration. In fact, their argument implies that the act of penis-vagina sex—an act that does not lead to orgasm for the vast majority of women—is more essential to the definition of

[35] Girgis, George, and Anderson, "What is Marriage," *Harvard Journal of Law and Public Policy* 34 (2012), 267.

[36] Girgis, George, and Anderson, "What is Marriage," 257.

marriage than even procreation.[37] For they are willing to allow a marital exception for infertility, but not for penis-vagina sex.

What Is Marriage?

Opponents of marriage for same-sex couples worry that without sex difference, marriage is redefined to merely an emotional bond with little distinction from friendship. They argue that relying on only emotional connection creates societal instability. Families are more likely to break-up if marriage is only based on emotional intensity. That is true, but they fail to note that heterosexuals have already implemented that redefinition. Sex difference did not stop that from occurring. Moreover, they recognize that marriages without procreation carry deep significance. Certainly, infertile couples ground their marriage in more than transient feelings.[38]

Scripture defines marriage as covenantal kinship of mutual support that typically includes the goods of procreation, sexual stewardship, and sanctification.[39] A distinction between

---

[37] "Less than a third of women are reliably orgasmic with vaginal penetration" (Emily Nagoski, *Come as You Are* [New York: Simon and Schuster, 2015], 274.

[38] Plus, sex difference by itself does not seem more likely to hold couples together than an emotional connection. In fact, no-fault divorce laws demonstrated that biological parents are often not willing to stay together even for their children. The question is why opponents of marriage equality don't expend more energy on restoring tighter divorce laws.

[39] Kinship is the purpose of marriage, while procreation, sexual stewardship, and sanctification are typical goods of marriage. **Kinship:** "It is not good that the man should be alone, I will make an *ezer* as his partner" and "bone of my bones, flesh of my flesh" (Gen 2:18, 23; 29:14; 2 Sam 19:12); **Procreation:** "God created humankind in his

the *purpose* of marriage and resulting *goods* of marriage is helpful to the discussion.[40] Kinship is primary. Procreation cannot occur before a kinship union is established otherwise children would be conceived out of wedlock. Similarly, sexual release prior to covenant falls into fornication. And, sanctification is the result of an existing marital covenant as the couple learns self-sacrificial love.

While Genesis 1 indicates God created sexual dimorphism for the *blessing* (and not mandate) of procreation, Genesis 2 and other biblical texts describe marriage as first and foremost kinship. This kinship is established by covenant and symbolically sealed in the act of sexual intimacy. God saw that it was not good for the human being to be alone. God saw that the human being needed a fellow ally (*ezer*). Bone of bone and flesh of flesh is kinship language (e.g. Gen 29:14). This is what distinguishes marriage from friendship, not just procreation. Kinship is a different kind of relationship than friendship.

---

own image, in the image of God he created them, male and female he created them. God blessed them and God said to them, 'Be fruitful and multiply . . .'" (Gen 1:27–28a); **Stewardship of Sexual Desire**: "But because of immoralities each man is to have his own wife, and each woman is to have her own husband . . . if they do not have self-control let them marry. For it is better to marry than to burn" (1 Cor 7:2, 9; NASB); **Sanctification**: "Therefore be imitators of God, as beloved children, and live in love, as Christ loved us and gave himself up for us, a fragrant offering and sacrifice to God . . . In the same way, husbands should love their wives as they do their own bodies. He who loves his wife loves himself. For no one ever hates his own body, but he nourishes and tenderly cares for it, just as Christ does for the church" (Eph 5:1, 28–29).

[40] I am grateful to colleague Rev. Cameron Merrill for pointing out to me the helpful category distinction between purpose versus goods.

Sex is not merely for the purpose of offspring but the covenantal act of kinship.[41] This is why Elkanah can say to his infertile wife, Hannah, "Am I not more to you than ten sons?" (1 Sam 1:8). In this statement, Elkanah affirms that marriage has great importance apart from procreation. In fact, he suggests the spousal relationship *by itself* is ten times more meaningful than having children.

This is confirmed by the meaning the biblical authors give to the marriage between God and human beings. God's marital covenant with Israel is: "I will take you as my people, and I will be your God" (Exod 6:7; see also Gen 17:7; Jer 30:22). The *relationship* between the two is the essence. When Christ marries his bride, the church, as described in Revelation, this sentiment is reiterated: "And I saw the holy city, the new Jerusalem, coming down out of heaven from God, prepared as a bride adorned for her husband. And I heard a loud voice from the throne saying, 'See, the home of God is among mortals. He will dwell with them; they will be his peoples, and God himself will be with them" (Rev 21:2–3).

Throughout Jewish and Christian tradition, the Song of Songs has been interpreted as a love allegory between God and humankind. This love story does not mention children. Rather the point is the relationship itself. Song of Songs describes sexual longing that fosters and encourages this bond. Surprisingly, the biblical authors were not shy about referring to our relationship with God in sexual terms.

Paul tells Christians to have sex (*kollaō*) with God, not sex (*kollaō*) with a prostitute (1 Cor 6:16–17). The word *kollaō* is associated with the term *proskollaó* in Genesis 2:24 (Greek translation), describing a man leaving his family of origin to

[41] The existence of the clitoris also indicates non-procreative purpose, along with positive health enhancing hormones that result from sexual activity.

cleave to his wife. In making this connection, Paul indicates sex is about covenantal bonding and carries spiritual meaning beyond procreation. Our ability to cleave to God, who is not sexually differentiated, implies that sexual intimacy metaphorically transcends sex difference.

Marriage Defined by the Familial Drive

The familial drive dictates that all of us are meant for kinship in order to flourish. It defines us as human beings. Kinship is about covenant, the relationship where we practice the virtue of life-long loyalty and commitment to another person with whom we are in unbreakable union. The beautiful symbol of Christ's relationship with the Church is iconic of the highest virtue, *chesed* (loyal lovingkindness). This very lack of loyal love in general, and not merely in marriage, has led to the debilitating social fragmentation we see in America today. *Chesed*, and therefore, kinship is essential for the well-being of every person, married or not.

Throughout much of history the idea of mass quantities of people living single lives in their own isolated apartments or in temporary, serial relationships would have been absurd. People married and had children, remained with extended family, or lived in a monastery or convent. They lived within kinship networks that were permanent and lifelong. There has never been a time in history when so many people were single and disconnected from permanent household.

It is no surprise that people are feeling increasingly lonely and isolated. In 1940 only 7% of Americans lived alone. By 2009 the number increased to 25%.[42] That statistic is now

---

[42] Johannah Cornblatt, "Lonely Planet," *Newsweek* (2009), https://www.newsweek.com/lonely-planet-isolation-increases-us-78647

edging toward 30%.[43] From 1985–2004, the number of people who said they have no one with whom to discuss important matters tripled. If that were not enough, studies demonstrate a link between social isolation and health problems.

When Christians sell books and preach sermons encouraging unmarried people to embrace their "singleness" as a blessing we are promoting the destructive effects of the sexual revolution—a movement that breeds impermanent relationships. Hook-ups. Divorce. Co-habitation. Serial lovers and roommates. "Singleness" in our culture is not the will of God at all. It is representative of a deeply disconnected society. Singleness often means a person lives alone or in non-permanent, non-kinship relationships. In other words, our culture is suffering from significant fragmentation as a result of a lost understanding of kinship, a lost understanding of covenant, loyalty, and commitment.

This is not to say that some people are not called to celibacy or that unmarried people cannot have a fulfilling life. Jesus was unmarried, and he never lived alone. He went from the family home to a group of twelve close friends who shared daily life with him until he died. His mother and brothers were also still involved in his life and are often mentioned. Jesus' mother was there at his darkest hour. But Jesus also died young around the age of 33, and his unmarried state, like Paul's, was unusual. Celibacy served a special ministry purpose that both men felt convicted they were called to and empowered to undertake.

Most people are compelled by the familial drive toward marriage. As Martin Luther observed, when we ignore this powerful God-given drive, it comes out sideways. It comes

---

[43] Ray Suarez and Eric Klinenberg, "Why More Americans Are Living Alone," *PBS* (2012), https://www.pbs.org/newshour/show/why-more-americans-are-living-alone

out in a culture of serial lovers and transient community. We are designed to leave our mother and father and cleave with another person to create a new family unit.

Family is different than friendship. It is life-long, covenantal, shared household. It is waking up next to the same person every morning and together carrying the burdens and joys of daily survival. In marriage we have the freedom of affection that even the best friendships do not have. Oneness of bodies not only releases bonding hormones that benefit our health, but it provides a physical security deeper than the hug of a friend. In marriage we care for our spouse's body as if it is our very own.

The Goods of Marriage

Kinship is the purpose of marriage, which is established by covenant and symbolically sealed in the act of sexual intimacy. But there are also goods that typically come with marriage, including procreation, sexual stewardship, and sanctification. These goods of marriage are often present, but not always. For example, an infertile couple will not experience the good of procreation, though they might adopt. Similarly, our bodies are subject to ailments, disability, and hormonal changes that can affect long-term sexual intimacy. Perhaps the one good of marriage that is most enduring is sanctification, although even here a person might develop a condition like dementia rendering them incapable of self-sacrificially giving to their spouse anymore. But despite the ebb and flow of these marital goods, the purpose of marriage—the kinship bond—remains until death as long as both partners honor and cherish covenant.

While procreation and sex difference are often touted as the premium goods of marriage, Scripture points to sanctification as the greater good. God says to Israel, "I will betroth you to Me in righteousness and in justice, in lovingkindness and in compassion, and I will betroth you to Me in faithfulness. Then you will know the Lord" (Hosea 2:19-20; NASB). Indeed, the original Abrahamic covenant was to sanctify a people to be a blessing to the nations: "Abraham will surely become a great and powerful nation, and all nations on earth will be blessed through him. For I have chosen him, so that he will direct his children and his household after him to keep the way of the Lord by doing what is right and just" (Gen 18:18–19).

The theme of virtue is reiterated when God's marital covenant is renewed with Israel through the prophets Moses ("You shall be for me . . . a holy nation"; Exod 19:6) and Jeremiah ("I will put my law within them, and I will write it on their hearts"; Jer 31:33). In the New Testament, Christ purifies his bride (Eph 5:25–27; see also Rev 19:8). For that reason, Paul urges spouses to imitate Christ by caring well for one another (Eph 5). We are all, male and female, predestined to be conformed to the image of Christ (Rom 8:29). In this way marriage is a witness to God's generous love. In as much as we love our spouses well and publicly, we are a living icon to God's faithfulness to us. Virtuous Christian marriages are a light to the nations, a means of evangelism to turn people's hearts toward God.

Conclusions

Throughout history people have been motivated to marry for a variety of reasons, whether for survival or companionship. While procreation is closely associated with marriage, this is by default. Historically, heterosexual sex has often inevitably resulted in procreation. But natural outcome need not mean required (indeed, use of modern contraception already makes that assumption). Genesis 1 indicates God created sex difference for procreation, and procreation is a *blessing* not an iron hand. Scripture affirms the legitimacy of marriage apart from procreation.

Kinship is the *purpose* of marriage, while procreation is a *good* that can result from marriage. This kinship is distinct from friendship in its covenantal commitment, which is symbolically sealed by sexual intimacy. While love between friends can be just as strong as between spouses, the unity of marriage physically, emotionally, and spiritually is distinct. It is borne out of the familial drive to leave one's family of origin to create a new kinship unit. It is the place for properly stewarding our sexual passions. And it is where we can practice self-sacrificial love on a daily, life-long basis in ways unlike any other relationship. The result is a profound witness to the world (and ourselves) of God's love for humankind.

Afterword

Wisdom invites us to help sexual minorities to participate in the purpose and goods of marriage in as much as they are able to do so. It makes little sense to prevent gay and lesbian people from forming kinship, stewarding their sexual desires within covenant, and experiencing the sanctifying effects of marriage simply because they cannot procreate or have penis-vagina sex.

Allowing the small minority of same-sex couples to participate in covenant will not change the societal eco-system. The overwhelming majority of people will continue to be predominately attracted to the opposite sex and desirous of procreative unions. Mercy for a minority with atypical sexual development does not replace or disparage the marital goods available to those with typical sexual development.

6

Is the Nashville Statement Biblical?

On August 25th, 2017, several conservative evangelical leaders gathered to hammer out the Nashville Statement during the annual Ethics and Religious Liberty Commission (ERLC) Conference, which took place in Nashville, Tennessee this year. The Statement was a joint endeavor of the ERLC and the Council on Biblical Manhood and Womanhood (CBMW). Modeled after the Chicago Statement on Biblical Inerrancy (CSBI), the manifesto expresses concern about homosexuality and "transgenderism," stating: "Our true identity, as male and female persons, is given by God. It is not only foolish, but hopeless, to try to make ourselves what God did not create us to be."[44]

In response, progressive Christians have offered various alternatives, including the Denver Statement and A Liturgists Statement. I want to address the question of whether the Nashville Statement is biblical, as well as comment on progressive responses.

[44] "Nashville Statement" (2017), https://cbmw.org/nashville-statement/

Biblical Interpretation and the Nashville Statement

The Nashville Statement cannot be understood apart from the Chicago Statement on Biblical Inerrancy (CSBI). If you want to thoughtfully engage the Nashville Statement, brush up on CSBI. Like CSBI, the Nashville Statement is formatted into several sets of affirmations and denials (fourteen in total) and named after the city in which it was drafted. The ecclesial intent is also the same: a litmus test for who is in and who is out. Those who don't sign will be obvious. This could affect who is hired, fired, or what ministry partnerships are formed.

However, the difference between now and the early days of CSBI is that evangelicals are more diverse. While CSBI was quite influential at one time, today the document is primarily upheld by those on the more conservative end of the spectrum. I suspect less evangelicals will rush to sign the Nashville Statement.

But, the more interesting question is whether the Nashville Statement is biblically sound. The writers subscribe to the biblical hermeneutics of the Chicago Statement. I highlight a few pertinent beliefs here:

1. *When writing Scripture, the biblical authors were in a perfected state akin to pre-fall Adam and Jesus.* CSBI Article IV states: "We further deny that the corruption of human culture and language through sin has thwarted God's work of inspiration."[45] At first, this sounds like an ordinary acknowledgement of the Bible's inspiration. But, R. C. Sproul's authorized commentary on CSBI clarifies: "Adam, before the fall, may well have been free from proneness to error, and Christ, though

[45] "The Chicago Statement on Biblical Inerrancy," ICBI Conference, Oakland, 1978,
https://library.dts.edu/Pages/TL/Special/ICBI_1.pdf

fully human, never erred . . . with the aid of divine inspiration and the superintendence of the Holy Spirit in the giving of sacred Scripture, the writings of the Bible are free from the normal tendencies and propensities of fallen men to distort the truth."[46]

By comparing the biblical authors to Jesus, the Bible is treated less like a collaborative effort between God and human beings, and more a product of a mechanical dictation view of inspiration. The drafters of CSBI would deny a dictation view, but that is the functional outcome, including downplaying cultural influences in the Bible.

That means followers of CSBI are more apt to subscribe to cultural concepts of the time period in which the Bible was written alongside Scripture's unique Christian tenets.

Notably, they often subscribe to a 1st century patricentric family structure as described in Paul's day. John Piper suggests a lack of adherence to hierarchical complementarian views of men and women (women in a submissive role) has caused "destructive consequences" that include the affirmation of same-sex relationships.[47]

2. *Modern scientific discoveries are not necessarily evidence of truth.* CSBI Article VII states: "We deny that Biblical infallibility and inerrancy are limited to spiritual, religious, or redemptive themes, exclusive of assertions in the fields of history and science. We further deny that scientific hypotheses about earth history may properly be used to overturn the teaching of Scripture on creation and the flood."

---

[46] R. C. Sproul, *Explaining Inerrancy: A Commentary* (Oakland: ICBI, 1980), 5.

[47] John Piper, "Precious Clarity on Human Sexuality: Introducing the Nashville Statement," *Desiring God* (2017), https://www.desiringgod.org/articles/precious-clarity-on-human-sexuality

In other words, Scripture is not just a theological book, it teaches infallible scientific truths that should be embraced above any modern scientific discovery should there be a contradiction between the two. That is why most adherents to CSBI believe a global flood occurred despite scientific evidence to the contrary, and why many still believe the earth is 6,000 years old or deny evolution.

In his commentary on this Article, R. C. Sproul states: "[W]hatever the Bible teaches about creation and the flood cannot be negated by secular theories."[48] However, he reluctantly allows that sometimes we must go back and re-read Scripture more accurately when science is irrefutable, such as with Galileo (albeit, irrefutable is subjective).

What this means in the current debate on same-sex relationships is that biblical statements about God creating male and female will override scientific discoveries related to sexual development.

Same-sex attraction or gender identity concerns are attributed to psychological or spiritual problems that a person must remedy with proper counseling and repentance. Or if the issues cannot be resolved, one must spend life fighting and suppressing those realities while viewing them as consequences of the fall.

3. *Scripture speaks with a unified voice; we should not make too much of multivocality in the Bible.* Article VIII states: "We affirm that the text of Scripture is to be interpreted by grammatico-historical exegesis . . ." One aspect of this approach, as described in the Chicago Statement on Biblical Interpretation (a supplement to CSBI), is no valid interpretation can "suggest that one passage corrects or militates against another" (Article XVII). All of Scripture is assumed to speak with a unified voice. So even though the biblical

[48] Sproul, *Explaining*, 16.

authors describe various types of marriage (e.g. multiple wives, levirate arrangement, rapist-victim nuptials) these are downplayed to propose that Scripture reveals one view on marriage.

The grammatico-historical approach also favors literary interpretation that is skeptical of historical-criticism. The socio-cultural world behind the Bible is not as important as the narrative in the text. The Chicago Statement on Biblical Interpretation states: "We deny that the distinction between the universal and particular mandates of Scripture can be determined by cultural and situational factors. We further deny that universal mandates may ever be treated as culturally or situationally relative" (Article VIII).

Understanding key interpretive assumptions that undergird the Nashville Statement is important for grasping its logic. The issue is more than just the valuing of sex and gender. After all, many progressives agree that male and female are meaningful and procreation is a beautiful gift. Rather conservative evangelicals hold additional presuppositions about the nature and function of Scripture that lead to limited options for addressing the complexity of sexuality. In fact, interpretive methods of CSBI can result in wooden interpretations that don't adhere to its own tenets of allowing Scripture to interpret itself. Scripture teaches us biblical mandates cannot be applied blindly.[49]

The Nashville Statement is also weak in the area of practical theology. The adherents give advice based on an idealistic world that does not exist. Everyone is expected to fit into the binary of male and female and heterosexual orientation. The preamble of the Nashville Statement reads: "It is not only foolish, but hopeless, to try to make ourselves what God did

---

[49] For discussion see chapters 4–6 in Karen R. Keen, *Scripture, Ethics, and the Possibility of Same-Sex Relationship*.

not create us to be." But this ignores the reality of actual human bodies that come into the world at birth in non-typical ways. It also dismisses (even mocks) the suffering many sexual minorities have experienced trying, in vain, to become cisgender heterosexuals.

The Nashville Statement acknowledges "physical anomalies or psychological conditions" and Jesus's reference to "eunuchs born that way," but the only suggestion provided is that such individuals should not think of themselves as such (Articles 5, 6, 7). They should instead have a "self-conception" of a perfectly formed male or female heterosexual. Where any ambiguity exists, one "should embrace their biological sex insofar as it may be known." This assumes, for example, that an intersex person is not *really* intersex. They just need to investigate a little further to determine whether one is actually male or female. That flies in the face of what intersex bodies are, compositions of male and female traits.

Similarly, the Nashville Statement implies that those who are gay or transgender can be healed. Same-sex attractions are the result of sin (Article 9) and such attractions can be "put to death" (Article 10). The theological language could refer to not acting on those desires rather than reorientation, but certainly many conservatives would read it as healing, especially when used with language like "transforming." Also implied is that same-sex attraction in of itself is sin. That means a gay person is perpetually in a sinful state by virtue of one's sexuality.

For those who are transgender, Article 13 states "the grace of God in Christ enables sinners to forsake transgender self-conceptions." Continuing to have a transgender self-conception is against God's will (i.e. sin). Yet, whether it's possible for a transgender person to conceptualize themselves in the way demanded is highly questionable. It is not simply an issue of mind over matter. If becoming a cisgender heterosexual was that easy, suicide among LGBTQ people would not be a problem.

The framers of the Nashville Statement essentially mandate the denial of one's body and adoption of a "self-conception" that is contrary to reality. That includes those who are transgender, as the brain is part of the body. The demand prevents honest acknowledgement of even documented congenital conditions. It provides no guidance for how people are to live the Christian life with the bodies they have, and instead proposes an imaginary idealistic world that results in unrealistic expectations.

Progressive Responses to the Nashville Statement

Any response that does not take the time to learn the presuppositions underlying the Nashville Statement will merely talk past the issues. While it might feel good to vent, thoughtful engagement with conservative evangelicals requires addressing deeper issues such as the relationship between science and the Bible. And it requires a respectful, charitable spirit. The problem with some of the progressive responses to the Nashville Statement is that they are hastily written reactions that equally fail to provide a robust Christian theology of sexuality. That does not mean they are entirely problematic; they are seeking to encourage and protect marginalized people like a mama bear protecting cubs. So, what I critique here is not progressive responses in their entirety, but specific aspects that I hope progressives will take into consideration.

A Liturgists Statement says, "We believe all people have full autonomy over their bodies, sexual orientations, and gender identities, and the diversity of identities reflects the creative power of a loving God."[50] What does it mean to have

---

[50] "A Liturgists Statement," *The Liturgists* (2017), https://theliturgists.com/statement

autonomy over our own bodies? Do the Liturgists understand this as something like pro-choice bodily autonomy? If so, I am not clear on the connection, as the writers of the Nashville Statement did not issue a call for the criminalization of same-sex relationships. They published a doctrinal position. How does the Liturgists Statement's assertion of "autonomy" interact with Scriptural theology such as, "Do you not know that your body is a temple of the Holy Spirit within you, which you have from God, and that you are not your own? For you were bought with a price; therefore glorify God in your body" (1 Cor 6:19–20).

A Liturgists Statement also says, "God is honored in any consenting and loving relationship between adults, and therefore, all such relationships deserve honor and recognition." *Any* such relationship? Does this suggest any non-marital sex outside of a covenanted relationship is holy as long as both people care about each other? Ignatius of Loyola taught that all of us should first seek God's will for our lives before even assuming that marriage is part of our life's vocation. The idea that God is glorified by whatever sexual relationship I consent to as long as it is loving has no theological depth. I know the Statement is intended to provide brief affirmations and denials, but still.

The Denver Statement is also found wanting. It reads: "We affirm that God created us as sexual beings in endless variety."[51] Can we assert, scientifically, that sexuality has "endless variety"? Certainly, variety exists, but endless? *Really*? Just as the signers of the Nashville Statement can ignore science, progressives can do the same, making sweeping statements about

---

[51] "The Denver Statement," *Sarcastic Lutheran* (2017), https://www.patheos.com/blogs/nadiabolzweber/2017/08/the-denver-statement/

sexuality that don't accord with what we can reasonably assert from research.

We do not have to completely deconstruct sex and gender or deny any meaningfulness of male and female to acknowledge that variety exists or to declare a space at the table for those who don't fit the norm.

The Denver Statement also falls short with its ironic judgmental tone: "We deny any self-conception that presumes one is capable of knowing God's holy purposes for other people" and "We deny that the grace of God in Christ sanctions self-righteous assertions of absolute knowledge of God's will."

The Denver Statement itself makes the kind of assertions it says it denies. It presumes to know absolute truth about God's will on sexual expression. The Statement also refers to "backward thinking," implying that the writers of the Nashville Statement are primitive and intellectually inferior. That doesn't go very far in positively influencing the conversation.

What progressives need to do is take more than twenty-four hours to formulate a statement. And it should avoid the pitfalls of the Chicago and Nashville Statements by bringing together global and ecumenical voices. Moreover, it should show some thoughtful engagement of what it means to think Christianly about sex and sexual relationships. One progressive document that offers an example is "A Theology of Marriage including Same-Sex Couples: A View from the Liberals." This essay begins with:

> Marriage is a discipline and a means of grace for sinners and for the whole church. It is a discipline because its vows are for better or worse. It is a means of grace because it signifies the love of Christ for the Church. We argue that the church should marry same-sex couples because it requires their testimony to the love of Christ and the church, and

because it recognizes that same-sex couples stand in need of sanctification no less than opposite-sex couples do. [52]

---

[52] Deirdre Good, et al., "A Theology of Marriage including Same-Sex Couples: A View from the Liberals," *Anglican Theological Review* 93 (2011): 51–87.

7

Infeasible Celibacy: Quotes from Christian Tradition

Discussion of Christian sexual ethics naturally raises the question of celibacy. Specifically, is life-long celibacy a viable option for every person or only for those with a unique capacity for it?[53] Can or should it ever be mandated? Below are comments from Christian thinkers across history on the infeasibility of life-long celibacy for most people.

Paul the Apostle (c. 10–60s). Paul championed celibacy, believing an unmarried life allows a person greater availability for ministry. But despite his positive view of permanent abstinence, he did not believe it was feasible for everyone, conceding, "If they do not have self-control [sexually], they should marry" (1 Cor 7:9; NASB).

Ambrose of Milan (337–397). The church fathers and mothers often considered celibacy superior to marriage, even to the point of encouraging married couples to cease having sexual

[53] A thorough discussion of celibacy and feasibility can be found in chapter 6 of Karen R. Keen, *Scripture, Ethics, and the Possibility of Same-Sex Relationships*.

relations, particularly after child-bearing years. Sex and sexual desire were deemed tainted by the fall. Yet even church leaders who extolled life-long virginity, did not claim such a commitment was feasible for all people. Bishop Ambrose wrote, "For virginity cannot be commanded, but must be wished for, for things which are above us are matters for prayer rather than under mastery."[54] He further states, "I do not discourage marriage, but recapitulate the advantages of holy virginity. The latter is the gift of few only, the former is of all."[55]

John Chrysostom (347–407). Long before the Protestant Reformation challenged the prevailing view that celibacy is superior to marriage, church fathers were already interpreting Paul's statement in 1 Cor 7:9 as scriptural evidence that life-long abstinence is not possible for everyone. Chrysostom observed, "Do you see the strong sense of Paul how he both signifies that continence is better, and yet puts no force on the person who cannot attain to it; fearing lest some offense arise?"[56]

Augustine (354–430). Augustine believed that celibacy is superior to marriage, even though he found practicing abstinence

---

[54] Ambrose, *Concerning Virgins* 1.5.23 in *Some of the Principle Works of St. Ambrose,* Nicene and Post-Nicene Fathers, Second Series, vol. 10, ed. Philip Schaff and Henry Wace, trans. H. de Romestin, et al. (Oxford: J. Parker & Co., 1896), 367.

[55] Ambrose, *Concerning Virgins* 1.7.35. Translation in Ariel Bybee Laughton, "Virginity Discourse and Ascetic Politics in the Writings of Ambrose of Milan" (Ph.D. Diss., Duke University, 2010), 90.

[56] John Chrysostom, *The Homilies of S. John Chrysostom, Archbishop of Constantinople, on the First Epistle of St. Paul the Apostle to the Corinthians,* trans. John Henry Parker (London: F. and J. Rivington, 1854), 248.

difficult. After sending away his partner of fifteen years, apparently at the demands of his mother who wanted him to have a lawful wife rather than a concubine, he found a second concubine to fulfill his sexual desires while waiting for his betrothed to come of age. Ultimately, he broke his betrothal to become a priest.

Yet, concerning marriage, he counseled, "For for this purpose are they married, that the lust being brought under a lawful bond, should not float at large without form and loose; having of itself weakness of flesh that cannot be curbed, but of marriage fellowship of faith that cannot be dissolved . . . Therefore married persons owe one another not only the faith of their sexual intercourse itself, for the begetting of children, which is the first fellowship of the human kind in this mortal state; but also, in a way, a mutual service of sustaining one another's weakness, in order to shun unlawful intercourse."[57]

Thomas Aquinas (1225–1274). Aquinas examined the question of life-long celibacy by looking to Scripture. He noted that Paul speaks favorably of permanent abstinence, but surmised that the apostle cannot have had in mind all people because that would result in the cessation of procreation and discontinuation of the human race. That in turn would prevent the full number of people elected for salvation to come to pass.

He interpreted Paul to prefer celibacy only for specific individuals and not all people simultaneously: "He tells the reason why he permitted marriage as a concession, namely, because each one has not received from God so much virtue

[57] Augustine, *On the Good of Marriage* 5-6 in *St. Augustin: On the Holy Trinity, Doctrinal Treatises, Moral Treatises,* Nicene and Post-Nicene Fathers, First Series, vol. 3, ed. Philip Schaff, trans. C. L. Cornish (Buffalo, NY: Christian Literature, 1887), 401.

as to enable him to practice total continence, as the Lord himself said: 'Not all men can receive this saying. . . He who is able to receive this, let him receive it' (Matt. 19:11, 12)."[58]

Aquinas likened the gift of celibacy to the parable of talents; some have been given five talents, while others might have only two. In other words, each person has different abilities when it comes to sexual abstinence (Matt 25:15; Wis 8:21). He concludes, "[B]ut each one has his own gift; as if to say: not everyone has received from God the gift of continence. Hence he says, if they cannot exercise self-control, that is, if they have not yet received this gift, they should marry, that is, be joined in matrimony: 'I would have younger widows marry' (1 Tim. 5:14). Then he gives the reason, saying, it is better to marry than to be aflame with passion, that is, be overcome by concupiscence."

Martin Luther (1483–1546). Luther stands out for his vocal opposition to life-long celibacy. He argued that becoming a Christian does not mean we cease to be human beings with bodily functions, including a procreative drive. "Much as chastity is praised, and no matter how noble a gift it is, nevertheless necessity prevails so that few can attain it, for they cannot control themselves." He also considered human sexuality to be fallen and "therefore because of this very disease, marriage is a necessity for him and it is not in his power to get along without it. For his flesh rages, burns and fructifies just like that of any other man, unless he helps and controls it with the proper medicine which is marriage."[59]

---

[58] For Thomas Aquinas's discussion and the two quotes in this section, see *Commentary on the Letters of St. Paul to the Corinthians*, no. 332–335, trans. Fabian Larcher (Emmaus Academic, 2012).

[59] Martin Luther, "Commentary on 1 Corinthians 7" in *Commentaries on 1 Corinthians 7, 1 Corinthians 15, Lectures on 1 Timothy,*

John Calvin (1509–1564). Like interpreters before him, Calvin understood 1 Cor 7:9 to mean Paul says celibacy is not feasible for all. Jesus's words were also interpreted this way. "Paul here expressly declares, that everyone has not a free choice in this matter [of celibacy], because virginity is a special gift, that is not conferred upon all indiscriminately. Nor does he teach any other doctrine than what Christ himself does, when he says, that 'all men are not capable of receiving this saying' (Matthew 19:11). Paul, therefore, is here an interpreter of our Lord's words, when he says that this power has not been given to all—that of living without marriage."

Calvin denounces those who make vows of life-time celibacy arguing that they are ignoring the instructions of Paul and even Christ himself. He concludes, "Virginity, I acknowledge, is an excellent gift; but keep it in view, that it is a gift. Learn, besides, from the mouth of Christ and of Paul, that it is not common to all, but is given only to a few. Guard, accordingly, against rashly devoting what is not in your own power, and what you will not obtain as a gift, if forgetful of your calling you aspire beyond your limits."[60]

Puritan William Gouge (1578–1653). While Puritans have a reputation for being prudes, they did not shy away from recognizing human need for sexual relations (albeit in belief that sexual desire is the result of the fall). "No sinne is more hereditary [than sexual passion] . . . Of all the children of Adam that ever were, not one to a million of those that have come to

Luther's Works 28, ed. Edward Sittler (St. Louis: Concordia, 1973), 25–31.

[60] Both quotes are from John Calvin, *Commentary on Corinthians*, https://ccel.org/ccel/calvin/calcom39/calcom39

ripeness of years have been true Eunuches [i.e. celibate} all their life time." [61]

Westminster Larger Catechism (1647). The Reformation's perspective on celibacy followed in the steps of a long, pre-existing tradition holding that life-long abstinence is not possible for everyone. But many Protestants went a step further to say that *any* person who makes a vow of celibacy is not only foolish, but also sinning against God. In fact, merely delaying marriage is deemed grievous. The Presbyterians declared, "What are the sins forbidden in the seventh commandment? . . . entangling vows of single life [Matt 19:10-11], undue delay of marriage [Cor 7:7-9; Gen 38:26]."[62]

Mother Mary Francis, PCC (1921–2006). What about views on celibacy today? Even Catholics who esteem celibacy, far more than Protestants, recognize human limitations. Mother Mary Francis emphasizes the importance of careful selection for those interested in joining a religious order, which requires a vow of celibacy: "'An outstanding gift of grace' is Vatican II's description of the chastity that religious profess (PC, no. 12) . . . When the 'outstanding gift of grace' that is religious chastity has not been given by God, there are certainly going to be multiple problems for the one who professes celibacy." She writes that such a vow requires "a force beyond and above nature" and that only those who show evidence of receiving this supernatural force or 'outstanding gift of grace' should be admitted to a religious order.[63]

---

[61] William Gouge, *Of Domesticall Duties* (London: John Haviland, 1622), 210.

[62] Westminster Larger Catechism, Q. 139.

[63] See chapter 5 in Mother Mary Francis, *Chastity, Poverty, and Obedience: Recovering the Vision for the Renewal of Religious Life* (San Francisco: Ignatius Press, 2007).

Focus on the Family's *Boundless* magazine (2009). Conservative evangelicals are also on record denying the possibility of life-long celibacy for everyone who attempts it. In fact, early marriage is often encouraged as a remedy: "God designed most of us to get married. . . at a certain point it becomes spiritually dangerous and even unhealthy to deny sexual relations. . . Just because our culture seems to think it's fine to wait until you're nearly 30 years old to take this step doesn't mean you should ignore what you know is obvious: God designed you for sexual relations; God limits all sexual activity to marriage; and if you're finding it difficult to control yourself sexually, He gives clear advice: Find somebody to marry."[64]

Mark Regnerus (1971–). Mark Regnerus, a Christian sociologist, wrote the following for the evangelical magazine *Christianity Today*: "I am suggesting that when people wait until their mid-to-late 20s to marry, it is unreasonable to expect them to refrain from sex. It's battling our Creator's reproductive designs."[65]

Albert Mohler (1959–). Albert Mohler, a prominent conservative evangelical leader and president of Southern Baptist Theological Seminary has promoted early marriage to protect against promiscuity: "The vast majority of Christians who have gone before us would surely be shocked by the very need for a case to be made for Christian adults to marry . . .

---

[64] Gary Thomas, "Marry Sooner Rather Than Later," *Boundless*, March 13, 2009, https://www.boundless.org/relationships/marry-sooner-rather-than-later/

[65] Mark Regnerus, "The Case for Early Marriage," *Christianity Today*, July 31, 2009, https://www.christianitytoday.com/ct/2009/august/16.22.html. Emphasis in the original.

Our bodies are not evolutionary accidents, and God reveals his intention for humanity through the gifts of sexual maturation, fertility, and sexual desire. As men and women, we are made for marriage."[66]

---

[66] Albert Mohler, "The Case for (Early) Marriage," *Albert Mohler,* August 3, 2009, https://albertmohler.com/2009/08/03/the-case-for-early-marriage/.

8

What I Learned about Dating

Do LGBTQ people have anything to teach the church about godly dating? What comes to mind when you hear the words "dating" and "gay" in the same sentence? Many of us have been exposed to negative stereotypes of LGBTQ people as inherently promiscuous and dysfunctional. In this chapter, I offer a Christian perspective on dating as someone who is gay. It provides insight into unique challenges LGBTQ people have faced with dating and marriage as a result of societal rejection, but it also offers a conversation starter on the topic of dating in general. What does ethical Christian dating look like?

Throughout history most LGBTQ people have not had the opportunity to experience and practice normal dating and marital rituals. That remains the case in many parts of the world, including conservative communities in the West. This reality significantly impacts the kinds of relationships LGBTQ people have. That is true regardless of where one falls on the theological spectrum—traditionalist or progressive. (Traditionalists often find themselves in relationships at some point despite their convictions.)

During my 20s I had four relationships with women (at different times). All of them were a source of spiritual turmoil as I did not believe God blessed same-sex relationships. I did not intend to violate my conscience. But like many young people, gay or straight, I had difficulty living out my convictions. I longed to love and be loved. Not only was I struggling with confusion over how a good Baptist girl could be gay in the first place, but I was not prepared for how to grapple with my unexpected sexuality.

After much struggle I eventually achieved consistent chastity by age 29, leading to more than seventeen years of celibacy—difficult years to be sure, but also ones characterized by much peace and joy that comes with living out one's convictions. Perhaps most surprisingly, all my years of celibacy have provided great clarity about dating. They allowed me to step back from the drama of romance to reflect on my experiences and what it means to have healthy. godly relationships in general. In turn, those insights prepared me to reenter the dating world a few years ago, after becoming theologically affirming.

It has been refreshing to approach dating from a much more mature place than my 20s. In this essay, I share what I have learned in hopes it might be helpful to some of you.

1. Overcoming shame is possible but may take time.

The amount of shame and self-loathing I felt in my 20s nearly killed me. Based on what I had been taught about gay people in my conservative Christian culture, I believed God and others viewed me with disgust and contempt, particularly in my failed attempts at chastity. Many of us from conservative backgrounds have learned troubling views about sex: It's dangerous. It's the worst thing you can do if you are not married. You will be scarred for life because of broken "soul-ties." Add to these messages the fact that I had sex outside of marriage *with a woman,* and, well, the results were predictable. I was so guilt-ridden and distraught I contemplated suicide and pleaded with God to kill me.

It's astonishing to me now that I believed non-marital sex is so grievous that I should *die* for the offence. If only I could have wrapped my arms around my younger self and reassured her of her worth. I would have told her that having sex outside of marriage—even with a woman—is not the worst thing in the world. I would have told her that the only lasting scars I have are the memories of intense shame and despair. While break-ups were painful, that pain passed and memories of former intimacy do not trouble me in the way I was taught they would. I would have told her that God loves her profoundly and wants her to live. And that is true even if she is messing up.

Internalizing God's love, not just intellectually, but in my heart, freed me from shame.

At the same time, when I became affirming many years later, I experienced a temporary resurgence of shame and internalized homophobia. My years of singleness and holding to a traditionalist view shielded me from ever having to deal with the social ramifications of being publicly coupled with a woman (my previous relationships were all closeted). It took me a couple years to grapple with the vulnerability of that. But, thankfully, I now feel more comfortable in my own skin than any other time in my life. I made a 180-degree turn from my younger days when suicide seemed like the only way out.

If you are struggling with shame, take heart. It *does* get better. You are beloved. Truly. Even if you are struggling to maintain your convictions, remember that nothing can ever separate you from the love of God. God's grace is greater than you can possibly imagine.

2. It's okay to learn by trial and error.

Qohelet ("the teacher") who authored the book of Ecclesiastes learned by trial and error. He wrote:

> I said to myself, "Come now, I will test you with pleasure" . . . I explored with my mind how to stimulate my body with wine while my mind was guiding me wisely, and how to take hold of folly, until I could see what good there is for the sons of men to do under heaven the few years of their lives. I enlarged my works: I built houses for myself, I planted vineyards for myself . . . All that my eyes desired I did not refuse them. I did not withhold my heart from any pleasure (2:1-4, 10; NASB).

Qohelet engaged in a highly experiential search for insight into the best way to live life. It was through trying things out that he gained wisdom to discern what was life-giving and what was vanity. This is not a message I learned in church. To make an error was simply bad. Period. One should avoid mistakes at all costs. Often in Christian circles, little opportunity exists for people to speak as freely as Qohelet and to ponder how we can learn from our experiences, including failures.

Some of the things I learned by trial and error in my romantic relationships:

• *Admiration of someone's gifts and abilities is not the same thing as love.* I got caught up in one relationship because I was enchanted by her alto voice and song-writing abilities.

• *Sexual desire is not the same thing as love.* I jumped into another relationship because of physical attraction. At the time, I had difficulty realizing that I was driven primarily by lust and not love. I assumed the strong feelings meant love.

• *The "idea" of a relationship is not the same thing as love.* Many of us deeply long to find a partner to share life and home with. That hope can be intoxicating such that we are more attracted to the possibility than the person in front of us. This especially happens when we don't know someone well and our imagination fills in the gaps, projecting all our dreams of the future onto them.

• *"Falling in love" is misleading.* I was truly in love with two women I was involved with. But looking back now, I see that they were not the right marital fit for me. I allowed myself to get swept away without asking hard questions about long-term suitability.

• *It's easy (and lazy) to allow feelings to be the primary guide to getting into a relationship.* It requires hard work to explore challenging and necessary questions about marital compatibility.

• *Going too deep too fast emotionally and physically can be hurtful.* Attraction is powerful, easily pulling us into relationships too quickly only to realize later a lack of compatibility. Dating is a means of getting to know whether someone is compatible, but pacing is important. Impatience is a red flag. If the relationship is meant to be, the connection will develop and persist without rushing it.

• *Dating is a teacher, helping us identify dysfunctional relational patterns.* I learned things about my interpersonal weaknesses and strengths that I never would have discovered otherwise. I learned how to identify unhealthy behavior in myself and others, making growth possible. Sometimes that growth came the hard way. It took getting the marrow sucked out of me in one relationship to cure me of co-dependency.

- *Sex makes it difficult to be discerning and clear-headed about the long-term viability of a relationship.* The bond sex creates can make us stay in a relationship even when it's not best for us.

- *Sinning sexually is not the end of the world.* Confess to God and mentors, then move forward.

When I reflect back on my relationships, I don't notice lasting harmful effects. I have not been scarred for life. Granted, I certainly made mistakes. Getting into a relationship out of lust and then breaking up with that person was a grievous thing to do, even if I was oblivious in my inexperience. It was sinful and calls for repentance. Similarly, I suffered the pain of rejection that took significant time to heal. Yet, I and the women I was involved with have all recovered and moved on. What has remained are the lessons I learned about what it takes to have a mature relationship. Paradoxically, past failure has enabled me to relate in more Christ-like ways precisely because of insight gleaned from those experiences.

3. Pursue transparency with all your heart.

One of the most, if not the most, significant barriers to healthy dating and marriage for LGBTQ people is secrecy. Shame prevents people from coming out. The closet is safe, but also the breeding ground of dysfunction. So many break-ups can be attributed to this. Secrecy means no accountability. The ability to share our crushes with friends, to get feedback from those who know us best about the person we are dating, to let others witness the dynamics of the relationship, and to make public vows of commitment are all essential to a healthy relationship. Without accountability it's easy to get into relationships that are not the wisest and easy to break commitments because no one will ever know or ask about it.

Lack of transparency can also impact opposite sex relationships. Many gay people have married heterosexually, hoping and praying that would fix their attraction to the same sex. Spouses have been left devastated by a gay husband's or wife's inability to love them holistically. Not uncommonly these mixed orientation marriages end in divorce.

Sometimes lack of disclosure in an opposite sex relationship is the result of shame that a gay person feels about their orientation. But lack of transparency can also result from denial. I dated men, believing my attractions to women were only a temptation, not an orientation. I was told if I prayed and practiced spiritual disciplines, I could fall in love with a man as God intended. When that didn't happen, and I had to break-up with these good men, the result was unnecessary pain and broken hearts.

As much as possible, we should seek to be transparent with ourselves and the person we are dating about our sexual orientation (or gender identity). But that is not enough. We also need to be honest with friends and family about our relationships. We need community accountability. Similarly, marriages are public because they need community to help sustain them. Secrecy will take its toll.

4. Discern whether you are called to marriage or celibacy.

Don't get into a relationship if you cannot in good conscience do so. Falling in love is incredibly powerful and makes us want to do anything we can to have that relationship. But if we are not fully resolved within ourselves that a same-sex relationship is blessed by God, it will lead to nothing but pain. Cognitive dissonance will usually end the relationship eventually. Don't hurt someone else by pulling them in only to break-up out of guilt. The same is true on the flip-side; even if we are personally okay with a relationship, we should not pursue those who still feel conflicted. We might be able to persuade them temporarily, but cognitive dissonance will often lead to mental health problems. Love them enough to let them go.

One phenomenon I experienced in my own life is that a traditionalist view of same-sex relationships as sinful can make it more difficult to be thoughtful about relationships. When I experienced strong mutual attractions, I avoided thinking too hard about it. I conflated honesty (about my feelings) with intentionality to sin. How could I admit to God and my church what I really wanted to do? I also felt less culpable if I just got swept away with my feelings than if I consciously planned for something to happen.

As a result, I never asked myself, "Is this person a good marriage partner for me?" I just jumped into the relationship, compelled by strong desires. Paradoxically, if I had been more intentional in planning my romantic relationships, it would have helped me to stay true to my convictions. I would have recognized that even though the attraction was compelling, I ultimately didn't want to spend my life with that person.

5. Ask good (hard) questions.

The euphoria of attraction can only take us so far. The infatuation will fade. The question is whether a person is actually a good, compatible mate. Don't wait until several months into a relationship when you are attached to ask important questions. If you are dating to find a spouse, but the other person is not willing or able to settle down, that is a good thing to know up front. There are plenty of books and tips out there for good questions to ask. But just to name a few:

• Are your relational values and sexual ethics compatible?

• Is your date willing to be out of the closet or do they want the relationship to be secret?

• Do they have peace that God blesses marriage for same-sex couples?

• Is their understanding of the meaning of marriage the same as yours?

• Are your personalities and lifestyles suitable to one another?

• Would the relationship draw you closer to God and God's purposes for your life?

• Are they relationally healthy and mature?

Don't short-change yourself and the other person if you recognize a significant incompatibility. That can be tempting to do when we so long to be in a relationship, but those incompatibilities will eventually become thorns.

6. Pursue true love.

I wish I had loved the women I was with more than I did. I wish I had loved them enough to avoid entangling them in a relationship I couldn't commit to because of my traditionalist convictions at the time. I wish I had loved them enough not to put my desires or infatuation before their well-being. I wish I had loved them enough to ask hard questions about marriage. I wish I had loved them enough to let them go. I realize some of my mistakes were the result of my own inexperience and confusion. But that doesn't excuse my hurtful actions.

Loving well means doing right by the other person. That may mean discerning a friendship is a better course to take with a particular person than dating. It may mean practicing self-control instead of prematurely starting a sexual relationship. It may mean not telling the other person about the attractions, for example, if they are already married or they are convicted to pursue celibacy.

True love means a Christian approach to dating and marriage. Ultimately, any relationship should draw both people closer to God. It should instruct us in selflessness. Godly marriage is a witness to God's faithful love for us. For that reason, sex and romantic love can never be casual. Passion is the kinship drive meant to compel us into covenant fidelity and oneness with another.

Addendum: Polyamory

My dating relationships have been monogamous, so I cannot speak to polyamory from personal experience. But I would be remiss not to mention it in a discussion on dating. Polyamory is increasingly a topic of conversation. While those of us in older generations might find it bewildering that it needs to be addressed, some young people, even in Christian circles, are exploring the option as a result of increasing societal acceptance.

Polyamory is a romantic or sexual relationship with more than one person. Most human beings naturally feel attracted to more than one person; that is a product of puberty. Thus, we could say that most people are polyamorous in their desires and capable of falling in love with more than a single individual. Finding a mate would be difficult without this ability. That is also why adultery can be a temptation. But polyamory in the dating world is not merely the recognition of this biological reality. It is the acceptance to act on that ability by becoming involved in consensual relationships with more than one person at a time.

Contrary to stereotypes, polyamory is not indiscriminate sex. Many polyamorous people adhere to serious ethical guidelines of consent and care. *But, importantly, polyamory is non-marital.* Polyamory may involve commitment, even long term, but that is distinct from marriage. Once polyamory incorporates covenant, it becomes polygamy. Thus, if one believes that marital covenant is the best context for sex, polyamory falls outside of a Christian sexual ethic.

However, this raises a secondary question: is polygamy a legitimate form of Christian marriage? The New Testament authors appear to have sided with Greco-Roman thinkers in adhering to monogamous marriage. But polygamy is not explicitly condemned in the Bible. In ancient Israel, polygamy appears to have fostered communal well-being if a wife was infertile and children were essential to survival, or a large number of men had been killed during war-time and women needed male support.

In many African countries, where polygamy has long been part of the social structure, Christians are less likely to be as troubled by the arrangement as Western Christians. Cultural factors can influence our perspective on whether or not polygamy is an ethical practice.

The reformer Martin Luther was not generally in favor of polygamy, but he also admitted that Scripture indicates it was permissible at times, as with the Israelite patriarchs. He discussed his views in a variety of sources, including letters to nobleman Philip of Hesse, a commentary on Genesis, and his treatise "The Babylonian Captivity of the Church." Luther suggested that, while polygamy should not be a Christian practice, marriage to a second spouse (bigamy) may be warranted on a case by case basis. For example, a man married to a woman who has contracted leprosy or another severe illness, preventing the couple from being together. He also urged a woman with an impotent husband to pursue a second secret marriage. He advocated secrecy for bigamy so as not to normalize it in the general population, but not because he believed it was always sinful to take a second spouse. Luther was not alone in his views. Several of his colleagues, including prominent theologian Melanchthon, likewise offered approval on a case by case basis.

Traditionally, polygamy has been male-centric. In fact, it would be more accurate to refer to polygyny, the practice of men marrying more than one wife. Luther's encouragement of more than one spouse for a woman is unusual. Usually polygamy has shown up in highly patricentric cultures and often relates to a desire for abundant offspring. In addition to catering to men's needs and accelerating procreation, polygyny (versus polyandry) is likely the result of a need to determine paternity. Polyandry—a woman taking more than one husband—is a practice that has been quite rare. Polygamy in a society that treats women equally and where paternity can be established by DNA tests would be a new territory.

So, what factors might be considered in the conversation on polyamorous dating?

- Polyamory is not marital. If one believes covenant is the best context for sex, polyamory falls outside of a Christian sexual ethic.

- Polygamy is not explicitly condemned in the Bible and is permitted in the Old Testament. Polygamy in antiquity and across cultures typically relates to offspring and community, not merely individual interests and desires. However, the New Testament authors utilize language that suggests preference for marital monogamy. Further investigation of Greco-Roman advocacy of marital monogamy and how that influenced Jews and Christians in the Second Temple period may be helpful for understanding the New Testament authors' sexual ethics on this question.

- Within Christian tradition, some theologians, including reformer Martin Luther, have considered bigamy ethically permissible on a case by case basis. These cases typically have to do with a severely ill spouse, inability to live out a sexless marriage (thus, temptation to fornication), or the need for offspring. A modern example might include someone whose spouse sustained a severe brain injury from a car accident, leaving the spouse with a developmental capacity of a six-year-old and altering the dynamics of the relationship from partners to parent-child.

With these factors in mind, as well as the principles drawn from other parts of this book, how might you address the issue of polyamory and polygamy (or bigamy) with young people today who have questions about dating and marriage?

9

Hermeneutical Principles 2

1. Legal deliberation is a hermeneutical approach used by the biblical authors to discern ethics.[67]

When encountering an ethical question, the biblical authors did not blindly enforce law. In fact, the Old Testament does not contain a comprehensive set of laws, as they were not meant to be read as such. The laws reflect principles of justice that were used as case law by subsequent generations to foster *deliberation*. Similarly, the New Testament does not give directives on many ethical concerns, particularly modern-day ones that didn't exist in antiquity. The biblical authors evaluated moral questions with attention to the circumstances at hand. They engaged in a deliberative process to determine whether or not to apply a scriptural mandate.

Reflection: *Do I read the Bible as a rulebook? If so, do I blindly apply rules without concern for the context of the situation at hand? Or do I take presenting circumstances into consideration when applying Scripture for ethics? Do I engage in a deliberative process?*

---

[67] For a comprehensive discussion see chapters 4–6 in Karen R. Keen, *Scripture, Ethics, and the Possibility of Same-Sex Relationships*.

2. General revelation (or natural revelation) can be illuminated through science, providing an authoritative source of truth on par with Scripture.

While scientists are not infallible, we can learn truth about God and the purposes of God from what we discover in God's creation. Throughout Christian tradition, theologians have studied the "book of nature" (i.e. the universe), alongside Scripture. R. C. Sproul, a well-known conservative evangelical leader, once said:

> I believe firmly that all of truth is God's truth, and I believe that God has not only given revelation in sacred Scripture, but also, the sacred Scripture itself tells us that God reveals Himself in nature—which we call natural revelation. And, I once asked a seminary class of mine that was a conservative group, I said, 'How many of you believe that God's revelation in Scripture is infallible?' And they all raised their hand. And I said, 'And how many of you believe that God's revelation in nature is infallible,' and nobody raised their hand. It's the same God who's giving the revelation.[68]

Reflection: *Do I accept general revelation as a source of authoritative truth? Why or why not? In what ways do I take into consideration general revelation, alongside special revelation (Scripture), when faced with an ethical question?*

---

[68] Keith Mathison, "Introduction: A Reformed Approach to Science and Scripture," May 4, 2012, https://www.ligonier.org/blog/introduction-reformed-approach-science-and-scripture/

3. Understanding the difference between descriptive versus normative ethics is important for interpreting Scripture.[69]

Descriptive ethics refers to the ethics of ancient Israelites and early Jews and Christians. It is the ethics of the biblical authors in their socio-cultural context. Normative ethics refers to how we apply Scripture for ethics today. Sometimes there is much overlap between the two. For example, we consider stealing immoral today, just as the biblical authors did. On the other hand, Paul instructed women to wear head-coverings in church, but today most churches have determined that directive was reflective of cultural practices in the 1st century and not a normative ethic for today.

Sometimes, descriptive and normative ethics are conflated together with the result that cultural practices from biblical times are prescribed today as if they were divine revelation. For example, some Christians enforce a patricentric family structure today, as seen in the Bible, believing it is a divine mandate, rather than reflective of culturally-based gender norms in antiquity.

Reflection: *Am I reading Scripture with an awareness of the distinction between descriptive vs. normative ethics? How do I determine when a practice in the Bible is reflective of the culture of the time period vs. universal morality that applies today?*

---

[69] For further discussion on this distinction see Andrew Mein, *Ezekiel and the Ethics of Exile* (Oxford: Oxford University Press, 2001), 6–12. See also John Barton, *Ethics in Ancient Israel* (Oxford: Oxford University Press, 2014) and Wayne A. Meeks, *The Moral World of the First Christians* (Philadelphia: Westminster, 1986).

4. A statement in Scripture can be descriptive rather than prescriptive.

This is similar to the distinction between descriptive vs. normative. But the nuance is more literary than socio-cultural. Just because something is *described* in the Bible does not mean it should be prescribed simply by virtue of appearing in Scripture. We are not meant to imitate everything we read in the Bible. For example, the Bible describes Hezekiah using fig cakes to treat a medical condition (2 Kings 20:7). That does not mean we should limit ourselves to biblical remedies for illness. Another example is Genesis 1–2. The Bible *describes* the creation of male and female, but this does not mean people with atypical sexual development don't exist. As Jesus acknowledged, some are "eunuchs who have been so from birth" (e.g. intersex people; Matt 19:12). Genesis portrays the majority experience rather than a comprehensive discussion of sexual development.

Reflection: *When I read the Bible, do I ask myself if a passage is descriptive vs. prescriptive? Have I ever assumed something was prescribed simply because it was described in the pages of the Bible?*

5. Sola Scriptura should not be confused with nuda Scriptura.

Sola Scriptura as defined by the early Reformers did not mean God's revelation *only* comes through Scripture and nothing else. The Reformers considered other sources of insight, including tradition. In fact, they frequently cited tradition to make their theological points. Today, many Christians who say they adhere to sola Scriptura actually believe in nuda Scriptura, which is the belief that Scripture and nothing else can reveal God's will. Only the Bible can be used as a source for ethics. In contrast, sola Scriptura is the view that Scripture is *primary* (prima Scriptura), while other sources can also aid in spiritual discernment (e.g. tradition or general revelation). Nuda Scriptura is a problematic distortion of sola Scriptura.[70]

Reflection: *Have I learned a distorted definition of sola Scriptura that prohibits any other source for insight and discernment? If so, how might I correct this by incorporating other sources, alongside Scripture, as conversational partners in ethical decision-making?*

6. The Wesleyan Quadrilateral provides one model for ethical discernment.

John Wesley was an Anglican who came to America to minister. From his work, the Methodist church was born. Anglicans draw from three key sources for discernment: Scripture, tradition, and reason, with Scripture primary. Wesleyans (or Methodists) are similar, but have added experience as a fourth source, creating a quadrilateral. More specifically, Wesley had in mind experiences involving the Holy Spirit. While Scripture is primary in Protestant tradition, most Christians, including Catholic and Orthodox readily incorporate other sources of discernment, as long as they do not contradict Scripture. It has been long recognized that trying to interpret and apply the Bible in a vacuum causes problems. It results in highly individualistic readings detached from anchors like tradition and reason.

---

[70] This problematic distortion is also recognized by conservative evangelicals: Matthew Barrett, "'Sola Scriptura' Radicalized and Abandoned," *The Gospel Coalition*, October 13, 2013, https://www.thegospelcoalition.org/article/sola-scriptura-radicalized-and-abandoned/

Reflection: *Have I ever considered the role of tradition, reason, or spiritual experience for ethical discernment? Why or why not? How might I incorporate these with Scriptural interpretation to shape my ethical conclusions?*

7. Scripture is best read for spiritual formation rather than as a rulebook.

The purpose of Scripture is first and foremost to tell the story of God's salvation and to point us to the Living Word, Jesus Christ. Much of the Bible is storytelling and relays the experiences the Israelites and early Jews and Christian had with God. The Bible is not meant to be read as a book of commands dictating every behavior. If that were the case it would fail to guide us because it cannot account for or predict the infinite ethical dilemmas that might arise. Instead, the Bible is best read as a source for spiritual formation. It teaches us the kind of people we are to be. As we are *formed,* we are equipped to make wise, ethical decisions.

Reflection: *Do I read the Bible primarily to give me commands to obey? Or do I read it to develop into a spiritually mature person who is capable of making wise, godly decisions?*

Further Reading on the Bible and Ethics

Lucas Chan, *Biblical Ethics in the 21st Century: Developments, Emerging Consensus, and Future Directions*

Charles Cosgrove, *Appealing to Scripture in the Moral Debate: Five Hermeneutical Rules*

Luke Timothy Johnson, *Scripture and Discernment: Decision-Making in the Church*

Karen Keen, *Scripture, Ethics, and the Possibility of Same-Sex Relationships*

Keith Mathison, *A Reformed Approach to Science and Scripture*

10

Ethical Framework Worksheet

This worksheet is designed to help you identify how you determine your ethics. It will take some time, so break it into manageable pieces and return as needed until you complete it. Most of us have absorbed ethical approaches without even thinking about it by the way we were raised or the culture we live in. To become a discerning person who seeks God's will, we can benefit from identifying our current ethical approach and whether or not changes are warranted.

Your ethical approach should be consistent and applicable to a broad range of ethical questions. Take your time going through each step below. The more specific you are, the more helpful the exercise will be.

1. What is your "baseline" for formulating ethics right now? Think about a recent moral decision you made (even a simple one) *not* related to sexuality. It could be something that happened last week at work or home. List the discernment steps you employed to arrive at your ethical conclusion. It may have been a subconscious or reflective decision that you didn't give much thought about at the time. But reflect on it now, break it down, and list the characteristics of your discernment process. What factors contributed to your decision?

2. Social location: What factors from your life have influenced how you determine right and wrong? Being aware of your social location can help you identify blind spots or subconscious ways you discern right from wrong. Likely, there are subconscious factors at play that you take for granted. For example, did your parents instill following rules without discernment ("Because I said so") or did they express reasons for their guidelines?

a. Consider *who* has taught you how to discern morality (e.g. parents, peers, clergy, teachers). What discernment theories and approaches have you accepted and rejected from these individuals? Be specific! What were you taught about the best way to achieve a virtuous life? For example, what did you learn about the role of emotions in cultivating a godly life? Or, what were you taught about handling relational conflicts? Write down the elements you currently accept. If you now reject a philosophy you were taught, rephrase/flip it into a positive statement that you do embrace.

b. How has *your place* in society influenced your approach to right and wrong? Contemplate socioeconomic status, educational level, race/ethnicity, gender, nationality, ability. For example, those who grew up in poverty might have a different ethical philosophy than those born into wealth based on their life experiences. You also likely learned positive or negative ways to interact with people from different social locations than your own.

3. Culture: What have you learned about discerning right and wrong from culture? This is similar to the social location question, but different. Specifically, what have you been taught about the *role* of culture in cultivating a virtuous life?

Is it good, dangerous, neutral? What principles for an ethical/virtuous life have you adopted from cultural influences? How do you determine which cultural ideals to accept or reject?

4. Experience: How have your life experiences shaped how you discern God's will? What principles for ethics did your experiences teach you? For example, have you learned from trial and error? Has pain or tragedy influenced your ethical outlook on life? What about exposure to other people's stories? Be specific (or indicate if you don't believe experiences influence your moral framework for discernment and decision-making).

5. Tradition: What Christian traditions have shaped the principles you live by? What current role does Christian tradition play when you are faced with an ethical problem? For example, do you read what the early church fathers and mothers teach about a particular topic to give you insight? Why or why not? How do you determine which aspects of tradition you accept or reject? *Note: Engaging with tradition is crucial for avoiding a myopic view that fails to learn from history. Yet just because it's tradition doesn't automatically make it correct.*

6. Reason: What role does human reasoning play in your ethical approach? Some Christian traditions emphasize that God's ways are above reason or that the fall has affected our ability to engage in virtuous reasoning. Do you agree or disagree? Does scientific discovery help inform right and wrong for you? In what way, if any, is science a form of God's natural revelation and, therefore, truth to abide by?

Interlude #1

Before moving forward, review your answers to questions #2–6. Take some time to look for patterns in your approach to ethics. Identify which specific sources of ethics you use for discerning the right thing to do. Synthesize your responses into a numbered list of steps you might take when faced with an ethical decision. Then, compare and contrast your list with your response to question #1. What elements do you want to carry forward? Make any adjustments to your list of discernment steps as needed.

7. Scripture: What role does Scripture play in discerning God's will for your life? This question is more involved because *how* we utilize Scripture for ethics makes a difference in outcome. Two people could say they rely on Scripture for ethics, but arrive at opposite conclusions. This question requires pondering your view and approach to Scripture (if you consider Scripture a source for ethics).

a. In what way is Scripture *authoritative* for you? *Sola Scriptura* = Scripture is primary, but other sources of insight (e.g. tradition, reason) are also relevant. *Nuda Scriptura* = no other sources outside of Scripture are applicable for discerning ethics (if you choose this option, consider if it contradicts your responses to questions #2–6). *Tradition + Scripture* = Christian tradition has *equal* authority as Scripture (Catholic and Orthodox view).

b. How much does the *socio-historical context* of the Bible matter for your interpretation of the Bible? Do you believe the "world behind the text" is just as important as the "world in the text"? Why or why not? How do you determine if something in Scripture is applicable today or only applicable to the ancient context in which the Bible was written?

c. What role does *history of interpretation or reception history* play in your study of the Bible? For example, do you read how other Christian theologians from antiquity or the Middle Ages have interpreted a particular biblical passage? Why or why not?

d. Richard Hays presents *four steps for utilizing Scripture* for ethics.[71] Would you follow his steps for interpretation? Why or why not?

- *Descriptive Task* – determining what a particular biblical author meant in his socio-historical context.

- *Synthetic Task* – discerning if a unity in ethical perspective exists across biblical texts/canon (Is there a consistent view across books and verses?)

- *Hermeneutical Task* – bridging the chasm between antiquity and now. (How do the biblical authors' views apply to a current ethical situation?)

- *Pragmatic Task* – embodying the Scriptures in everyday life.

---

[71] Richard Hays, *The Moral Vision of the New Testament: Community, Cross, and New Creation, A Contemporary Introduction to New Testament Ethic* (New York: HarperCollins, 1996). Note: Hays's book is a good introduction to biblical ethics. However, the crucial problem is that he avoids naming love as a guide for a New Testament ethic. This is in contrast to Jesus and Paul who say all the law is summed up in love of neighbor.

e. What role does *legal deliberation* have in your approach to Scripture? Do you believe it is acceptable to apply case law for extrapolating principles from Scripture that might not be explicitly stated or to revisit a mandate in Scripture? If the biblical authors engaged Scripture in this way (and they do), what are your beliefs about following that example? Are you permitted to do so? Why or why not?

f. If you turn to Scripture to answer a problem, *how do you study the text?* Do you do a topical study and look up all the related verses? If so, do you consider how different texts are written in different time periods? What about literary context or theological themes? What about archaeological or historical-critical approaches? In other words, what steps do you believe are best for studying the text to interpret and apply it well?

g. When you read Scripture for ethics, are you looking for a *rule to follow* or do you read Scripture for *character formation* that shapes you into a wise person who can then discern how to make a decision?

Interlude #2

Review your responses to question #7 on Scripture. Synthesize your response into a numbered list of steps that you will take when approaching Scripture for help in resolving an ethical question.

8. Character & Wisdom. Aristotle suggested ethics is first of all about our character and not first of all about decision-making.[72] Behavior or decisions are outcomes of our pre-existing character. What role does character currently play in your approach to ethics? How is character developed? How do you actively cultivate the fruit of the Spirit in your life? How does good character give you wisdom that informs your ethical viewpoints and decisions? What is the relationship between character development and other sources of ethical insight as described above?

Summation Exercise

Create three columns. In the first column place your list of steps from questions #7 and title it "Scriptural Insight." In the second column place your ethical discernment steps gleaned from questions #2–6 and title it "Other Sources of Insight" (only include sources you will actually use for informing God's will for your life). In the third column create a list of steps that synthesizes your response to #8 on character and wisdom and title it "Wisdom."

After you have created these three lists, contemplate how all three intersect for you. Give each column a percentage for how you weight them. In other words, if you consider all of them equally influential in discerning God's will for you in a situation, give them each 100%. If you consider one weightier than the others apply percentages accordingly.

Case Study: Sexual Ethics

Only after you have determined your approach to ethics should you proceed with determining your stance on an

---

[72] For a helpful summary of Aristotle's view see Richard Kraut, "Aristotle's Ethics," *Stanford Encyclopedia of Philosophy* (2018), https://plato.stanford.edu/entries/aristotle-ethics/

ethical question. Your ethical framework is intended to apply to a broad range of ethical questions. A lack of consistency in your approach might signal a blind spot that affects sound judgment.

Review your three columns of listed steps. Go through each step of each column to inform your discernment on the question: "What is the proper context of sex for the godly Christian?" Be specific about who, with whom, and when.

About the Author

Karen R. Keen is a biblical scholar, author, and spiritual director. Founder of the Redwood Center for Spiritual Care and Education, she has taught biblical and theological studies in both academic and church settings. Keen earned her M.S. in education (counseling) from Western Oregon University, M.A. in exegetical theology from Western Seminary, and Th.M. in biblical studies from Duke Divinity School.

Other Books by Karen R. Keen

Scripture Ethics and the Possibility of Same-Sex Relationships (Eerdmans, 2018)

"At a time when debates about the viability of same-sex unions for Christians often generate more heat than light, this marvelous little book by Karen Keen is a true gift. . . . Both at a head and heart level, *Scripture, Ethics & the Possibility of Same-Sex Relationships* is the most compelling, biblically-based, and scientifically informed case for the church to accommodate covenanted same-sex unions that I have ever read." — Gregory A. Boyd, pastor, author of *Letters from a Skeptic* and *Cross Vision*

"Karen Keen here provides a needed, integrative perspective that fruitfully brings together evangelical biblical interpretation, theological ethics, and pastoral wisdom to frame a loving, Christ-honoring discussion about same-sex relationships. This is a very helpful resource for seminary students, pastors, and congregations." — Elaine A. Heath, professor at Duke Divinity School, author of *God Unbound: Wisdom from Galatians for the Anxious Church*

Take the Class

This course reader was specially designed for "The Bible and Sexuality" class taught by Karen R. Keen. Visit the Redwood Center for Spiritual Care and Education to find out how you can register.

redwoodspiritualcare.com

"Karen is a gifted teacher and Bible scholar. I would highly recommend this course to anyone who wishes to deepen their understanding of the Bible and sexuality." — Rev. Dr. Michael Norrie, chaplain

"Karen's facilitation skills created a brave and compassionate learning environment that invited honest questioning and conversation. At a time when people can feel overwhelmed, intimidated, and alienated by conversations regarding Scripture, ethics, and sexuality, Karen's course offers a refreshing and stretching environment to explore one's beliefs in the context of a charitable learning community." — Lee Kosa, lead pastor at Cedar Park Church

"Iron can't sharpen iron in isolation and Karen creates safe and knowledgeable space for such a dialogue. I would highly recommend this class." — Gil Vollmering, Jr., church elder and parent of a gay son.

CPSIA information can be obtained
at www.ICGtesting.com
Printed in the USA
LVHW111029280721
693933LV00011B/162